The Essence
And Preeminence of
SONSHIP

The Essence
And Preeminence of
SONSHIP

PETER AKECK

authorHOUSE®

AuthorHouse™ UK Ltd.
1663 Liberty Drive
Bloomington, IN 47403 USA
www.authorhouse.co.uk
Phone: 0800.197.4150

To contact the author, kindly write to:
Apostle Peter Akeck,
Pioneer Apostolic Ministries,
P.O.Box 1507,
Kakamega 50100,
Kenya.
Tel: +254 722 257 681
Email: petakeck@yahoo.co.uk

Published by AuthorHouse   05/22/2013

ISBN: 978-1-4817-8745-1 (sc)
ISBN: 978-1-4817-8746-8 (e)

Unless otherwise indicated, all Scripture quotations are from the King James Version, The Hebrew-Greek Key Study Bible © copyright 1984 and 1991 Spiros Zodhiates and AMG International.

Dedication

This book is dedicated to all humanity regardless of nationality, colour, creed, occupation, religious persuasion or position in society; who seek a life of fulfillment beyond being just full in life.

To those in authority, leaders, parents and ministers of the gospel and especially those who have the responsibility and opportunity to teach and raise others.

To my precious children, Jannet Blessing and Paul John Galligan, who joyfully gave away their time with dad during the time of writing this book.

To all who call me dad.

You all inspired the writing of this book.

Contents

FOREWORD

TO "THE ESSENCE AND PREEMINENCE OF SONSHIP" by Peter Akeck.

I first met Peter Akeck in his home town in Western Kenya in 2002. We ministered in the church fellowship where Peter was an assistant pastor. We spent some time together and Peter took us to a photocopy shop and it was there that he asked us to lay hands on him, because he felt called to the apostolic ministry. We saw Peter again in 2003, and ministered in the local church where he was.

Peter came with us on team to Rwanda in 2004, and it was there that we commissioned him to the ministry of an apostle. Ever since that time Peter has walked in relationship with us and has been an integral part of the host team in Kenya. We have been privileged to minister in Kenya every year since 2000. Peter was ordained as an apostle of Jesus Christ in 2007 in his home apostolic company in Kakamega, West Kenya.

Peter has always been a brother who picks up on revelation very quickly. The Lord has quickened his understanding amazingly. On many occasions Peter has served me as my interpreter, and on occasion when another had been appointed as the interpreter, when Peter saw him struggling to pick up on the things that I was sharing, Peter would offer to relieve that one, and then the word would really flow.

I have thoroughly enjoyed reading Peter's book, "The Essence and Preeminence of SONSHIP", and have received some wonderful insights that have added to my own faith and understanding. We have been predestined to become the sons of God (Eph.1:5), and it is by faith, that is, hearing the quickened word, that we actually become the sons of God (Gal.3:26). God's design has always been *"many sons to glory"* through Jesus Christ (Heb.2:10) and all of creation *"is eagerly waiting for the manifestation of the sons of God"* (Rom.8:19).

The message of sonship is one of the core messages of the apostolic restoration that God is bringing to pass in the earth at this time. God's goal is to present to Himself *"a glorious church"* (Eph.5:27). This is a body of disciples who have come to a place of maturity, having been presented by the Spirit to the Father to receive and walk in the inheritance (Rom.8:15-17; Gal.4:5-7). These are the sons whom the Father will chasten (Heb.12:5-9), so that we become fully conformed to His will, which is *"to be conformed to the image of His Son, that He might be the first born among many brethren"* (Rom.8:29).

I recommend this book and especially because it will help the reader understand and begin to walk in the reality of sonship.

Paul Galligan, apostle of Jesus Christ
Revival Ministries Australia
www.revivalministries.org.au

RECOMMENDATION

The "Essence and Preeminence of SONSHIP" is a book you do not want to miss reading.It is written by a man of God, a true chosen and sent apostle, who knows the daily glory of being a son of the FIRST BORN OF MANY SONS UNTO THE FATHER IN HEAVEN. After reading it and connecting with other powerful teachings I have received from him, my life and ministry have been thoroughly blessed and transformed.

Peter Akeck has been and is a spiritual father to me for many years and in this book he powerfully unveils the plan of the Father, who through the revelation of Jesus Christ, will raise up many sons unto glory of the Father and dominion in the earth. This book explains the Father's heart and the heart of a true son. I highly recommend reading it.

Rev Joan M. Cella
Newark, New Jersey,USA

Acknowledgments

To the God and Father of our Lord Jesus the Christ, for the Spirit of wisdom and revelation in the knowledge of Him.

To Apostle Paul Galligan, Toowoomba, Australia, a teacher and a father who developed the apostolic and grace upon my life. From you I first heard the clear teaching on the topic of sonship and impartation of the same, which brought me into the grace and walk as a son before the Father.

To Dr Jim Lindsey, Pa, USA, an apostolic Prophet and an awesome teacher of His word to the body of Christ in America, Kenya and the nations, with whom I have had the privilege to travel extensively in all the major cities, towns and villages of Kenya and Pakistan, training church and ministry leaders, for over five years. Your fellowship and friendship unfeigned have been indispensable to my life and ministry.

To Rev Joan M Cella, New Jersey, USA, a pastor, a daughter and a mom to me for over five years whose support, love, encouragement and faith made this book a reality.

Preface

The heart of God bleeds sonship. Never before in the history of all creation has God desired to be known as a Father than now, considering that it is to us that the ends of all things have come. The consummation of God's plan in the earth cannot be without this critical relationship between Him and earth.

Revelation precedes restoration and restoration precedes habitation. God is looking for a habitation; a habitation among men so that He may not only be found in His house all the time, but more importantly, that He might be revealed in and represented by His sons in the earth, all the time. The message of sonship is one of the many that has been roughly handled by some church leaders and used as a means to keep people in bondage to their cruel and unpolished styles. This is unlike the spirit of sonship which liberates and heals and encourages. God's promise at the end of the Book of Malachi stands now more clearly than ever:

> "Behold, I will send you Elijah the prophet before the great and dreadful day of the LORD: and he shall turn the heart of the fathers to the children and the heart of the children to their fathers; lest I come and smite the earth with a curse."
>
> Malachi 4:5-6

The Day Of the Lord, the day of His full revelation and manifestation, not only to His people but to all the earth, cannot come unless first of all there is in secure place, the restoration of father—son relationship.

Many are hurting today; pastors, leaders, teachers, apostles, prophets, evangelists, singers, ushers—name them—because their hearts have been bruised, their lives have been discouraged, their goals have been unrealized and their hopes have been dashed. They are still ministering but deep within them, there is a hollowness that the money, the gifts, the material acquisitions cannot fill.

Some of them look very full and successful and accomplished but deep in their souls, there is a leanness; a nagging, tormenting emptiness and dissatisfaction. They are using their fame and acquisitions as security and proof of their identity and security, but these cannot replace the genuine part missing, sonship. These are but simple signs of the curse that God said He will smite the earth with in the absence of true father—son relationship between Him and His people.

The question is; do you want to be full or do you want to be fulfilled?

I have had the privilege of travelling extensively and I have taught on this topic more than any other. From one city to another, from one nation to another, from one continent to another, the situation has been the same: a deep insecurity and slavery in the hearts and lives of even the most successful looking ones; deep longing for the Father and for placement as sons to this Father. God is a Father; that is where all relationship begins. Jesus taught us to pray to a Father in heaven. Jesus came to the earth to tell us about the Father and to draw us to this Father. In Him is our fulfillment and fullness.

Coming into this dimension of revelation and relationship with the Father is the key to unfolding the fullness of the Father, His glory, to cover all the earth as the waters cover the sea.

There cannot be any higher calling.

Peter Akeck, B Th, MCL, an apostle of Jesus Christ
Pioneer Apostolic Ministries International,
Kakamega,
Republic Of Kenya.

Chapter One

The Design For Sons

"God is a Father, and God is a Son. God is
a Father with a Son, and God is a Son with a
Father. God is a Father to a Son, and God is a
Son to a Father. The Father fully dwells in the
Son by design. The Son is the embodiment of
the Father,the housing in which the fullness of
the Father abides. The Son is the body of the
Father and the manifestation of the Father. To
see the Son is to see the invisible God. This is
the essence and preeminence of sonship."

There is a wisdom that resides in the domain of men; of
the rulers of this age and those that are highly esteemed
for who or what they are. There is a wisdom that has
generationally constructed adorable structures and left
behind breathtaking impressions.
Take for example the wisdom that Nebuchadnezzar
possessed and the matchless might he wielded in all
Babylon. Take the wisdom that built the huge sea faring
vessels. Take the wisdom that landed men on the moon
and spies the Mars. Take the wisdom that built some of the
wonders of the world.

This wisdom is documented and widely worshipped.
However, in God, there is another wisdom; a wisdom of
the Creator that reigns higher than the wisdom of this
world. It is the wisdom of God. In this wisdom, all other
forms and appearances of wisdom come to nothing.

> "Howbeit we speak wisdom among them
> that are perfect; yet not the wisdom of this
> world, nor of the princes of this world, that
> come to naught: But we speak the wisdom
> of God in a mystery . . . which God ordained
> before the world for our glory"
>
> 1 Cor 2:6-7

In this unparalleled wisdom, God initiated a design for the earth. It is of note to observe that the Bible in its entirety has a lot to say about the earth and God's plan for it than it does about heaven. In the genesis of the book of Genesis, after verse one, chapter one, verse two gathers all attention and draws it to the deplorable state and condition of the earth, in fact to the point of telling the reader that even the Spirit of God was brooding upon the face of the deep. That God, by His Spirit, was not sitting pretty in heaven some distance away, with folded arms enjoying the serenity of heaven while earth went to hell.

God's deep love, concern and plan for the earth gets unfolded in the eyes of the reader from the very beginning. In this divine design, God creates a man, issues a woman from his fullness and places them on earth. He created the first man—male and female—and placed them in the earth.

> "Male and female created He them; and
> blessed them and called their name Adam, in
> the day when they were created." Gen 5:2

This man, Adam, was both the male and female, and God gave to them a singular corporate name, Adam. Adam was their name. In the beginning there was no Adam and Eve. In the day that they were created, there was no Adam and Eve. Adam was their name; their sole identity and the perfect definition of their being. This was because in God's creational and manifestation order, the woman became the subsequent issuance of man, the manifestation of the man's fullness in the earth, the issue by which he shall fill all things.

Actually and on a very powerful note, the word for "help meet", as used in the King James Version is the Hebrew "neged", a word whose root is "nagad" which means "to front", "to stand boldly out opposite of . . . to manifest, announce, explain, predict, expose and worship." (This quotation is taken from The Hebrew Greek Key Study Bible, KJV, Copyright 1984 and edited by Spiros Zodhiates and AMG International, Inc.)

This makes the woman "one who stands boldly out opposite of the man to manifest, announce, explain, predict, expose and worship(submit to) the man. The picture of Christ and His eternal purpose for the Church cannot be made any clearer to us at this early stage of unfolding divine design.

Luke, in recording the most comprehensive genealogy of Christ, draws one of the most critical conclusions;

> "which was the son of Enos, which was the
> son of Seth, which was the son of Adam, which
> was the son of God." Luke 3:38

Luke saw the design for sons as something that did not visit God later in His plan implementation. Right from the beginning, Luke makes it clear to us that God created man, male and female, called them Adam and Adam was the son of God! Adam the son of God! Adam was created by God a son of God. The first piece of humanity that issued from God and was placed on the earth, was not a child of God, or a servant of God; but more importantly, was a son of God.

From the beginning, God had a plan to fulfill and a mission to accomplish in the earth. This entire plan would be vested on the sons of God. God's mission and plan has to do with His sons and not just servants or children. This must first be accurately construed because this comprehension lends purpose to all that he was created for.

Before we go further into what this son was created for or to be, let us take time and consider where this son was created. This is because it is where he was created that gives him meaning.

> "And God said, Let us make man in our image, after our likeness ..."
>
> Gen 1:26

God did not say, "Let Us make man our image", God said, "Let Us make man in our image."

So man was created, not the image of God, but *in* the image of God. The image of God therefore becomes the mold into which the form of man was designed, and after which man gets his form and definition. The mold that makes the brick gives the brick form and definition.

> "He is the image of the invisible God; the firstborn over all creation."
>
> Col 1:15

Christ, the Son of God is the image of the invisible God. Man was made in the image of God. Reading Gen 1:26 together with Col 1:15 brings the conclusion in Eph 2:10;

> "We are His(God's) workmanship (work of His hands), created in Christ Jesus unto good works, ..."
> (Brackets mine).

How interesting. God made His son in His Son. He created Adam in Christ. This is the key to Luke's authority and audacity to conclude that Adam was the son of God, and by extension, to our definition as sons when we are in Christ. The title "son" can only be appropriately used by those who have discovered themselves in the Son. It is the mold that gives form and definition to the vessel as the potter works on it. In all society, it therefore goes without saying, that man's fulfillment or lack of it, hinges on two properties, namely;

- Where he is
- Who he is.

The 'who we are' is derivative but not generic; it is the explanation and extension of the 'where we are'. Locations define occupations. Every occupant takes on the form and name of its location, because you cannot "be" where you do not fit. Environments define characters. Homes define moles. The prodigal son in Luke 15, lived in two worlds and had two identities. In a far country, he was a servant feeding swine, and, at home, he was a son feeding on the fatted calf. Where he was, created or recreated him; gave him a new name. That is why the first question that most significantly mattered to God at the fall of man was not what man had done or why he had done it, but was "where are you?"

> "Therefore, if anyone be in Christ, he is a new creature." 2 Cor 5:17

The environment of Christ redefines the creature that has just explored and been assimilated in it. Homes define moles. Coming into Christ restores man to his original mold in which he was created but walked out of in disobedience and rebellion—just like the prodigal son did—and gives him a new name. Christ is not just our mold of definition, he is our covering, our garment for identification for blessing.

The blessing with which God blessed His first sons in the Garden of Eden is the same blessing with which all the families of the earth get blessed in Abraham. It is also the blessing with which Christ affords those who are in Him. Every father characteristically blesses his son(s).

> "That the blessing of Abraham might come upon the Gentiles in Christ, . . ."
>
> Gal 3:14

For Gentiles to become sons, and heirs, they must be redeemed by Christ and, two, they must be in Christ. The divine design for sons displaces Isaac and replaces him with Christ as the "Seed" of Abraham (Gal 3:16).

The Gentiles (strictly, non-Jews) had no association whatsoever with Abraham, considering that the "clean" were not allowed to touch anything 'unclean" lest they became defiled. The Gentiles were alienated from the commonwealth of Israel and became strangers to the covenants of promise, without hope in this world and without God. Christ came in as the acceptable garment by which that which was unclean and unacceptable would eventually become clean and acceptable, just like the garment did to Jacob when he wanted to come to his father for a blessing that was not his.

> "For as many of you as have been baptized into Christ have put on Christ"
>
> Gal 3:27

Jacob knew he was not acceptable but Esau was, before their father. To come to the father and be acceptable, he had to come under a baptism, under a covering; the covering of the loved and acceptable one. He wore Esau's clothes on his body and a goat's skin on his arms, splashed Esau's cologne on himself and came to the father in the likeness and appearance of his brother. The father was blind; a picture of God who does not look as man sees. When he smelt him, the smell of his son Esau, the accepted one, drowned the offence of the unfavoured one and blessing came upon the face and life of Jacob, forever. So it is with us in Christ.

In Christ, we receive a new identity and we who were not a people now become a people because the Father can smell the gracious and gratifying fragrance of His beloved Son on us and accept us as He would His Son, as Christ. We have become acceptable in the Beloved. In His Son, He receives and accepts sons. This is the wisdom displayed in the first man, Adam.

Everything that God spoke to Adam, everything that God gave them, He did on the premise and basis of their sonship. This was the divine design; that He shall only deal with His sons on earth; that the connectivity between heaven and earth shall be His sons. Therefore, the first revelation that Adam had of God is of Father. He looked at all the Father had done and understood the essence and preeminence of sonship. All the promises that God made to him, he did on the understanding that Adam was His son.

To ring this in your ear and establish it in your heart and mind, we are going to deliberately remove the nouns 'man' and 'Adam' and pronouns 'he', 'him', 'you', 'them', 'their', and in their stead, deliberately place the word *'son'* and *'sons'*.

> "And God said, Let us make *sons* in our image, after our likeness: and let *sons* have dominion over the fish of the sea, and over the

> fowl of the air, and over the cattle, and over all the earth, and over every creeping thing that creepeth upon the earth." Gen 1:26

- God created sons to be in and to bear His image and to walk and work in likeness to Him. What this implies is that an appearance of God graced the soft grass of the earth in the form of man. God appeared on earth in man, in His son.

- God created sons and gave them dominion (the right and might to rule) over all the earth and its fullness.

Due to very high and competitive life stakes, and the seemingly insurmountable trials and challenges of this age, majority of the world's societal folk—be they in the high pedestals of economic, political or otherwise acclaim, or, be they in the humble stables of toiling for a living—all seek and toil to be full at whatever cost. The rich want to be a little bit more rich and the poor want to be a little less poor. In this complexion, every one is giving it their all, if in any eventuality, they shall be able to churn out a better life, full of what they need and want for many days to come, if possible, for ever. They seek to fill their stomachs and surround their lives with immense material cushion against the worst of times. All this is good for whatever it is worth. However, being full and filled does not necessarily mean that you are fulfilled.

> "And he gave them their request; but sent leanness into their soul."
>
> Ps 106:15

In the wilderness, they had all the meat and angels' food they wanted but their lives were deprived and emaciated by the hunger of destiny. They were unfulfilled. However, a fulfilled person enjoys all the fullness. Fulfillment is not in what you have or did; it is carefully designed in two perspectives we mentioned above, namely;

i)   Where you are

ii) who you are in where you are.

So, for starters, being filled is the mentality of servants and being fulfilled is the mentality of sons.

> "And God blessed *sons*, and said unto *sons*, Be fruitful and multiply, and replenish the earth, and subdue it: and have dominion over the fish of the sea, and over the fowl of the air, and over every living thing that moveth upon the earth."
> Gen 1:28

- God's blessing rested on His sons.

- God wanted His sons to be fruitful.

- God wanted His sons to multiply.

- God wanted His sons to replenish the earth.

- God wanted His sons to subdue the earth.

- God wanted His sons to exercise double dominion over all the fullness of the earth.

> "And God said, Behold, I have given *sons* every herb bearing seed, which is upon the face

of all the earth, and every tree, in the which is the fruit of a tree yielding seed; to *sons* it shall be for meat." Gen 1:29

- God chose and gave food to His sons

  "And the LORD God planted a garden eastward in Eden; and there he put the *son* whom he had formed." Gen 2:8

- God created a chosen home for His sons in the earth, in the direction and place of His right hand.

  "And a river went out of Eden to water the garden, and from thence it was parted, and became into four heads." Gen 2:10

- God nourished and conditioned His sons' environment, home, with His river.

  "And the LORD took the *son,* and put the son into the garden of Eden to dress it and to keep it." Gen 2:15

- God provided an assignment for His *son*; to dress (care for) and keep (preserve, protect) his environment, home.

  "And out of the ground, the LORD God formed every beast of the field, and every fowl of the air; and brought them unto *the son* to see what *his son* would call them: and whatsoever *the son* called every living creature, that was the name thereof." Gen 2:19

- God gathered and brought every created animal to His sons for determination of their identities for their destinies.

- God approved of and established the identities of all created animals as decreed by the word of His sons.

> "And the LORD God commanded the *son* saying, Of every tree of the garden, thou mayest freely eat:
>
> But of the tree of the knowledge of good and evil, thou shalt not eat of it: for in the day that thou eatest thereof thou shalt surely die."
>
> Gen 2:16-17

- God demanded willful obedience from His sons as the sons executed God's assignment.

- God freely allowed His sons to choose to do His will.

- God warned His sons of dire consequences if they disobeyed.

A brand new view and perspective dawns on us all when we read these powerful verses with the word '*son*.' From the very beginning, God only wanted His sons to be in the earth.

David writes in the Psalms and paints an awesome picture of the man whom God created. Again, we shall deliberately replace every 'man' and 'him' with '*son*'. By doing this, we are not only restoring the meaning but are also releasing the power of God's divine design.

So, David says;

> "What is the *son*, that thou art mindful of *sons*? And the son of *son* that thou visitest the *son*?
> Thou hast made the *son* a little lower than the angels,
> And hast crowned the *son* with glory and honour.
> Thou madest the *son* to have dominion over the works of thy hands; thou hast put all things under the *son's* feet."
>
> Psalms 8:4-6

David makes it clear that God visits His sons; He loves the fellowship of His sons.

The first two sons God created were crowned with glory and honour. God told them to multiply and replenish the earth. With what? With their children. If the father and mother are sons, what would the children be? Sons. God's divine design was to cover the face of the earth with His sons, and by extension with His glory and honour. Everywhere the sons of the sons would be, there the crown of glory, there the rulership and majesty of their parents would be. God wanted an earth and air filled with His glory and honour; the revelation of His fullness and His worship all over the earth. This was His divine design for having sons in the earth.

God created and crowned (finished and perfected and established) His sons with glory and honour.
God created everything for His sons, male and female, and spoke to all creation through His sons whom He had created. The marriage between heaven and earth was presided over by His sons. This is the divine design from the beginning.

However, instead of this intended marriage of all things in one, these sons chose a forbidden path that precipitated the miscarriage of God's design though for a season, when they willfully disobeyed their Father and consequently suffered loss.

The first thing they lost was their place; their placement as a son. Consequently, they lost all the privileges that came with sonship; glory, honour, dominion, home, decree, food, security, identity, ability to subjugate, rights, might, etc

> "For all have sinned and fallen short of the
> glory of God."
>
> Rom 3:23

Man fell short of the crown; the crown of glory and honour. He lost the crown because he had lost the throne.

This changed man drastically as he found himself outside the chosen, nourished home and in the outer worlds; worlds without design for his design, worlds un-designed for him and so unfit for his living. God chased him out of the home and blessings that came with it, but knew He would not survive out there and, that, while on the verge of perishing out there, he would make every attempt and effort to come back home. He therefore, instituted a formula for his prodigal son's grand comeback; for his total recovery and restoration.

The greatest and most crucial revelation of God that any generation can receive is of God as a Father. God raised men in the Old Testament, men like Abraham and David—two key characters in history upon whom the entirety of our being and promises hung—as fathers who were charged with the responsibility of revealing the fatherhood (heart) of God to all men in their generation and beyond. This is because God is first a Father, then a Saviour. He is first a Father, then a healer. He is first a Father, then a Deliverer, a Lord, a King, etc. Actually, all these other great titles simply talk of what He is and not who He is. He is a Father who does great wonderful things to men, and particularly who fulfills His wonderful promises to His sons. The divine design concerns a Father who lavishly and opulently visits the earth with His sons and says, "Come on boys, let us do this . . . , let's make a home here"

CHAPTER TWO

The Calling Of Sons

"For God so loved the world that he gave his only begotten Son that whosoever believeth in him should not perish, but have everlasting life."
John 3:16

God lost a son. He chose to send His Son to seek and find and restore His lost son back to the divine design. Those who are of the lost son but who believe in the sent Son are given power to become sons of God.

"But as many as received him to them gave he power to become the sons of God."
John 1:12

"But when the fullness of the time was come, God sent forth His Son, made of a woman, made under the law, to redeem them that were under the law, that we might receive the adoption as sons." Gal 4:4-5

"Behold, what manner of love the Father hath bestowed upon us, that we should be called the sons of God."
1 John3:1

"It was meet that we should make merry, and be glad: for this thy brother was dead, and is alive again; and was lost and is found."
Luke 15:32

> "having predestined us to adoption as sons by
> Jesus Christ to Himself, according to the good
> pleasure of His will."
>
> Eph 1:5 nkjv

Jesus came into the world to seek and save that which was lost. The sum total of that which was lost is sonship; its essence and preeminence.

The reason we are saved from the kingdom of darkness and conveyed into the kingdom of the Son of His love, is so that we may come back to the place; to the placement as sons in God's kingdom.

We were redeemed to receive our adoption as sons again to the Eternal Father. We were saved to become sons. We were saved to be taken back home, to our placement as sons before the Father, to walk in His divine design again.

The coming back of the prodigal son is not as important as to where he came back to. He came back home; to the place of the father for his re-placement as a son, the very thing he had lost and whose loss cost him everything. This is the whole purpose and essence of salvation. The evangelists must preach this message right and biblically, so that the new converts can begin looking forward to sonship instead of looking up for rapture.

The greatest reward to "he that overcometh" is;

> "shall inherit all things; and I will be his
> God, and he shall be my son."
>
> Rev 21:7

The hope and goal of our overcoming the persecutions and tribulations of this life is the full restoration into the fullness of the Father's revelation and our perfect placement and stay in Him as sons of the Most High.

As it was in the beginning of the Book, when God created all things for His sons, so shall it be at the end of it; His sons shall inherit all things.
So the Bible becomes a sonship Book from the beginning of creation to the consummation of all things. God is a Father and He is looking for sons in the earth. Sons of God are needed in the earth, but these sons are in bondage in the outer worlds and need redemption.

> "And their dead bodies shall lie in the street of the great city, which spiritually is called Sodom and Egypt, where also our Lord was crucified."
>
> Rev 11:8

The writer of the Book of Revelation brings up something very spiritual here. He boldly says our Lord Jesus Christ was crucified in 'Egypt'! He says that this 'Egypt' is not a nation or a country but a city and a great one. There is no city in the world called Egypt, and so this makes the allusion very spiritual. He further says that in the street of this city where our Lord was crucified, there also shall the bodies of the two martyrs lie; that the death that killed the Lord kills them too. This is very spiritual and must be spiritually discerned.

To begin with, this has nothing to do with the country in the north of Africa called Egypt, at least not now. This is because Jesus was not crucified in the country called Egypt. Because this is a spiritual city and a spiritual street, it is also a spiritual death and a spiritual Egypt. So now that we have read the words, we now need the message in these words. The word 'Egypt' is used here to refer to the system

17

that held the firstborn son of God in bondage and killed her destiny, thereby crucified the Lord.

> "And thou shalt say unto Pharaoh, Thus saith the LORD, Israel is my son, even my firstborn: And I say unto thee, Let my son go that he may serve me: and if thou refuse to let him go, behold, I will slay thy son, even thy firstborn."
>
> Ex 4:22

God's son, even His firstborn son, was in bondage in Egypt. Bondage is not home, is not where sons are placed. It is a place of suffering, of unfulfillment, of torture, of mourning and of oppression. It is a 'home' away from home. It is a false home designed to keep God's sons away from home, from true identity, from true Father, from true destiny.

This is the spiritual Egypt being spoken of in the book of Revelation. This 'Egypt' has kept God's sons in bondage, offering them alternatives which could not cause them to live the life of the Father. It killed God's witnesses and placed their bodies in the streets as a witness to all who would want to seek freedom.
But God's word is crystal clear to Pharaoh;

"Let my son go that he may serve me."

It is impossible to serve the Father in this 'Egypt'. It is impossible to be a son in this 'Egypt'.
It is time to call out the sons from 'Egypt', for the Lord says;

"Let my son go that he may serve me."

> "When Israel was a child, then I loved him, and called my son out of Egypt.

> As they (the voice of the prophets) called
> them (sons of God) so they (sons of God) went
> from them (Egypt and its systems) ..."
>
> Hos 11:1-2a (brackets mine)

Even today, God is calling His sons out of 'Egypt' called denomination, because 'Egypt' makes them into slaves and not sons.

What is this place spiritually called 'Egypt'?

'Egypt' is a spiritual system with variant manifestations with a mission to ensure God's sons never come forth to come up in the land.

It is that place where sonship cannot be realized.

It is any system that resists God's purposes of bringing many sons into glory.

It is a diabolically designed organization, denomination, an order, an institution, a ministry, whose mission is to keep God's people in blindness, waste their time and never allow them to come forth into destiny.

It is an organized plan to keep men full but not fulfilled.

So in 'Egypt', if you murmur, complain or become uncomfortable, they give you offers and dangle carrots before your eyes to pacify you. It has worked very well in many denominations, even so called spiritual churches, whereby saints are received and maintained as members, years upon years and never allowed to rise into maturity in the revelation of Christ and be released to become all that God created and saved them for.

When the Israelites were in Egypt, they ate so much and when they were in need in the wilderness, they began to scream with weird nostalgia;

O the onions, the garlic, the cucumbers, the meat we freely ate, the melons, the nice food . . . Oh"

They missed being full and cared nothing about moving on to fulfillment. Ask yourself; do you want to be full or fulfilled? Today, in all that you are caught up in, busy in the ministry and doing this conference and that seminar and running from place to place and here and there; are you getting full or are you getting fulfilled?

'Egypt' can offer you and give you anything as long as it keeps you ignorant and away from sonship to God. Infact, 'Egypt' can even promise you freedom! When the children of Israel came into Egypt, they were allowed to choose wherever they wanted to stay. The land was all before them. Little did they know they could choose any place but only within the borders. The promises of 'Egypt' are limited to its borders. It will never allow you to rise to become yourself in Christ.

'Egypt' *denominationalises* people and drains their vision and destiny. It kills witnesses of the Lord. It crucifies the Lord; it handicaps Him so that His will cannot be done. This is because His will is done through His sons and when His sons are in bondage, He is crucified.

Christ was crucified by those who hated him and His mission; both the apostolic and priestly mission. Therefore 'Egypt' is any of that system that resists the apostles and the apostolic revelation; those systems that resist the grace of God that brings salvation to all men, and offers alternative righteousness and way of church practice.

'Egypt' is a religious system that practices another word, is controlled by other books apart from the clear apostolic revelation. 'Egypt' insists that people must be under it, lords it over the people of God and uses them to further its own agenda. 'Egypt' uses the gifts of people and then abandons them when they become shells of their true selves. Egypt kills slowly but surely.

A large percentage of what is called church today is a very good example of 'Egypt', because most of what it is doing is hoarding people, not setting them in order and then setting them free. So pastors fight over church members and pray that none of their members leave their assemblies. Today it is with a sense of pride and self gratification, and not shame, that you will hear a pastor publically praise a leader serving under him: "we have been with this brother/sister for the last twenty years in this church. He is a very faithful one." Can you imagine somebody sitting under you for twenty years! Such a person is either already dead or planning to kill you. Jesus took three years and said, "Go ye therefore, . . .". The former is a clear example of what modern day 'Egypt' can do to precious people. Jesus' style is the true example of the church. Those assemblies are becoming modern day 'Egypt' and are crucifying the Lord having killed His witnesses.

Egypt offered Moses a name, a throne, an education, an inheritance. All these were in an attempt to kill the sons of God in 'Egypt' and frustrate God's eternal plan of bringing many sons to glory in the land.

'Egypt' can be full of miracles and power display, but it is still 'Egypt'. This is because 'Egypt' talks of works and not inheritance and freedom. The languages of 'Egypt' do not spell the word 'sonship.'

'Egypt' seeks to maintain the status quo, resists change into the newness of what God is saying. It is a place of slavery; slavery of vision, of dreams, of purpose, of callings, of potential, of identity and of hope.

You cannot become a son in Egypt. So God sent Moses and his team to Pharaoh with the message:

"Let my son go that he may serve Me."

It is time that the Father is calling His sons out of every 'Egypt' that they are in; that has impoverished their lives, robbed them of their destiny, kept them serving men and the Egyptian wishes. It is time for sons to come out so that they can eventually come forth in the earth.

'Egypt' is very intelligent and philosophical and knows how to keep strings on people so it can tag them anytime to make the people do its will. 'Egypt' makes you rich with its things so that you can use them to serve it.

It looks like a wicked large denomination where one individual sits above all the branches and has a string that pulls all the branches and controls their programmes and activities. Consider the example below:

"You cannot baptize others until we lay hands on you. We cannot lay hands on you until you have served with us for ten years. You cannot serve with us for ten years unless you have been to our seminary or college. You cannot join our college unless you are our member. You cannot be our member unless you pay and renew your membership fee every month. Until then you cannot break bread, you cannot preach, you cannot teach, you cannot dedicate children, you cannot marry, you cannot serve in this ministry."

That sounds like a typical 'Egypt' which kills the witness of the Lord; the apostolic teaching and practice, and by extension, crucifies the Lord.

'Egypt' may purport to have allowed you to serve God but it will never allow you to serve outside the copy it gave you, which essentially *denominationalises* you more and more. 'Egypt' makes you Egyptian, not Christian. To be Christian, you must heed the call of God and come out of 'Egypt'.

Today, many ministers of God, many wonderful men and women of God are dying in 'Egypt'. In 'Egypt', you will never know the Father. You will always have masters and Superintendents and teachers but never shall you come to rest. Rest is in the Father. The Father is outside 'Egypt'. His voice is calling,

"Come out of 'Egypt'!"

'Egypt' overworks and finally kills those it imprisons.

God's judgment is upon 'Egypt'. But like it was with Sodom and Gomorrah, God wants His sons out of it first. Remember both Sodom and 'Egypt' are spiritually used to refer to where the witnesses of the Lord and the Lord Himself were killed. These are spiritual systems powered by the devil to curtail and cajole the holy seed. God is judging them for holding back His sons.

It is time for sons of God to come out of 'Egypt' to enter into their placement and inherit all things.

> "Giving thanks unto the Father, which
> hath made us meet to be partakers of the
> inheritance of the saints in the light: who hath

> delivered us from the power of darkness, and hath translated us into the kingdom of his dear Son:"
>
> Col 1:12-13

Because most of the church has been in 'Egypt' for so long, it costs a lot to come out of 'Egypt'.

What It takes To Come Out Of Egypt.

- *The Appointed Time*

> "Now I say, That the heir, as long as he is a child, differeth nothing from a servant, though he be lord of all; but is under tutors and governors until the time appointed of the father . . . But when the fullness of the time was come, God sent forth his Son, made of a woman, made under the law, to redeem them that were under the law, that we might receive the adoption as sons"
>
> Gal 4:1-2, 4-5.

There is an appointed time set by the Father for us to step out of Egypt and its shackles and step into sonship. This divine time is set and occasioned by the *rhema* word.

Every time has a sign. Every time has a fullness. The sign of the times precedes the times and must be spiritually discerned. The fullness of the times supersedes the times and must be exploited. Jesus rebuked the Pharisees who boasted of being able to read the weather and predict the seasons. He challenged them because they could not tell the signs of the times of the Lord and as a result resisted Him, though He came in the fullness of His time.

Times have signs. The magi from the east came to Jerusalem in search for the King of the Jews because, they said, "We saw His star in the east". The star they saw was a sign of the time; the time the Messiah was born in the earth. David, though the anointed and legitimate King of Israel, waited until the time of divine removal of Saul. He did not force his way; he did not breakthrough to the throne. He prepared himself through warfare trainings in the wilderness while looking after his father's sheep. He trained men of war in the wilderness through hunger and cold. He then waited for the fullness of time, the time appointed for him to inherit the throne.

Allow me to say something here. Waiting for the appointed time is a means to maturity. God is not just interested in you getting it; He wants you to *have it with character.* Character is the sustainer of all that we receive. Those who can wait can get details. Moses took time even when he was told to go to Egypt and deliver God's firstborn. He took real time with God. Those who can wait can grow. Coming out of Egypt is one thing but handling the inheritance is another, so God gave them forty years of waiting until they were now ready to enter the land.

John the Baptist was hidden "in the wilderness until the times of his manifestation to Israel."

There is a time set for you to come out and move in. This time is very determining and hence worth knowing. God is not only interested in getting you out; He wants to get you out *well*, in one piece. By revelation we receive the word and spiritually come out of the system. That should not make you pre-empt divine preparations and arrangements going on to receive you out there.

Kicking and cursing those you work with just because you have caught this revelation, and banging on heaven for your breakthrough, is not wise and is most likely to spill into the new thing God is delicately working on in your life. Keep looking for the signs of the times. Like was the case with Jesus, there could be a Herod that has to die before you can safely come out.

> So Joseph, with Mary and baby Jesus were to "flee into Egypt and be thou there until I bring thee word."
>
> Matt 2:13

The ignition for actions of life is in the release of the word of and from God. This is the word of life that releases light to the paths of men so they do not stumble in the darkness in the society. This is because darkness cannot handle, overcome or control this light of revelation. The revelation of God is in the life of God. The life of God is in the word of God. (John 1:4-5)

When God speaks a new word, a new spiritual dimension and atmosphere is created in the heavenlies. Heaven, or better, the spiritual realm, gets impregnated with divine intents and contents, in readiness to invade and rule the earth, or better, the physical realm, in the appointed time. The causation of a new spiritual dimension aligns the earth to heaven, by unveiling a new season on earth that men and women of discernment need to discern and prepare the ground for. The causation of divine intents is occasioned by His timely spoken word. This word sets divine timings for the earth; it appoints and chooses special moments for fulfillment and occurrences.

You have to wait for that *rhema* word, that word that announces the time to come out. This is the voice of the

Son calling out His sons out of Egypt. Have you heard it in your spirit, in your inner man? Have you received the revelation?

> "And was there until the death of Herod: that it might be fulfilled which was spoken of the Lord by the prophet, saying, Out of Egypt have I called my son."
>
> Matt 2:15

The steps of a good man are ordered by the Lord and wherever they are, they are fulfilling something prophetic, even in Egypt.

So Joseph stayed put with his family in Egypt. The clock was ticking and the Child Jesus was growing up, probably even beginning to learn the Egyptian language and culture, but Joseph stayed put. He was to be there until God brought him word. The word of faith, the word for action had not come.

He did not fight for his breakthrough back to his legitimate possession, like most Christians have been taught to do. He did not fast for forty days to release the word. Spiritual warfare in the New Testament must be taught again in light of what we learn from the first apostles and how they dealt with challenges, opposition, resistance and forces of darkness. A lot of teaching on these issues has been based on the Old Testament without a correct interpretation and fulfillment in Christ, the Seal of the New Covenant.

Every piece of the armor of God mentioned in Ephesians chapter six is a dimension of the revelation of Christ. In short, we are being asked to 'put on Christ' or be baptized into Christ; not just in water. When all these dimensions are brought together, they constitute what apostle Paul calls 'the manifold wisdom of God' with which the church rises to manifest and challenge principalities and powers in the heavenly places. Again he makes it clear how this is done;

> "To the intent that now the manifold wisdom of God should be made known by the church to the principalities and powers in the heavenly places."
>
> Eph 3:10

This is what a mere deacon, but one who had sat under apostles and had been well instructed in apostles' doctrine did, and his action brought him into the fellowship of apostles; fellowshipping in the revelation of and with Christ in obedience to His instruction:

> "And Philip went down to the city of Samaria and preached Christ unto them"
>
> Acts 8:5 nkjv

The result was everybody's attention was arrested, unclean spirits came out of people, the bound were delivered, the chief witch of the city, Simon, was subdued and even tried to join the disciples. The fear and horror of witchcraft was broken and "there was great joy in the city." That is the power of practicing New Testament apostolic Christianity; doing warfare by the manifestation of the manifold wisdom of God, which causes the life of God, the word, to become the light of men. This light (hot revelation, present truth of Christ coming forth in our time) shines in the darkness of satanic domain, influence and territory, and darkness cannot comprehend; overcome, hold or control it. Glory be to God. I believe Paul had this in sharp focus when he first wrote to the church in Ephesus about the revelation of Christ in chapter one then warfare in chapters three and six.

We walk with the revelation of Christ. We war using the revelation of Christ. We do not invade towns and cities and villages looking for demons and evil spirits to fight. We are not tomb raiders and demon hunters. We are servants of Christ and stewards of the mysteries of God. We focus on the people with our ammunition and should the devil try to stand in the way, collateral damage—of himself, his team and his paraphernalia—cannot be underestimated. This is spiritual warfare strategy in the New Testament.

There are many things and many people and many situations God is preparing and aligning out there before He brings you word which brings you out of 'Egypt'. He does not want you to get out of 'Egypt' only to let you land in the belly of a more terrible 'Egypt' than the one you left. Many people who are seemingly but ignorantly running from 'Egypt' to protect the deposits of God in them, like Hagar, end up in confusion and like Hagar, cannot tell where they are coming from and where they are going. [In my book "Displaying Unquestionable Authority", I have fully dealt with this]. They end up in another ministry or church and before the dust settles down, they discover, to their amazement, they made the worst choice of their lives.

Out of shame, frustration and pride, they find it hard to go back to the frying pan. Eventually, they break away and start their own thing—just to be ventilated in freedom. This is because they realized that while it is true they moved from 'Pharaoh', they were still warped within Pharaoh's family tree; from father to son to grand son. We are not to move from Pharaoh to Pharaoh's son to Pharaoh's grand son. We are to move from faith to faith, from glory to glory; grace upon grace.

God is working out a situation out there to receive you and raise you up as His son. Wait for Him to bring you word.

His messengers are coming to bring you the word for your redemption.

On the other hand, do not procrastinate like Jonathan. Jonathan got the revelation but could not discern the time to shift loyalty. Allow me to interject here that when the time came for David to be made king over all Israel, even the tribe of Benjamin, from where Saul came, discerned the time and came to Hebron to join their brethren in making David king.

Jonathan knew perfectly well that the kingdom and glory had departed from Saul his father (a picture of 'Pharaoh'), and was now on David. His sword, belt and spear crossed over but himself he never did. He died fighting with and for the old system.

How painful it must have been to die with revelation just because one could not discern the signs of the times! He took too long to shift to David. Maybe he kept on saying, 'Tomorrow, I shall call it quits, forfeit my inheritance from dad and cross over to David. O no, after this particular battle that dad has, I will cross over.' He never crossed over because he never returned alive from that battle. His body lay side by side to his dad's. What a pity.

Do not wait too long and do not hurry. Seek apostolic counsel and the help of those who have gone through this and prayerfully make the step in the right timing, the appointed time.

So, from the time Moses came back to Pharaoh to the time they eventually came out of Egypt, a lot of precious time had gone by. Days, months had elapsed. God was resetting them mentally and physically. He was still revealing Himself to them as He was dealing with Pharaoh so that as they went out, they would know whom they were dealing with and never would they take Him lightly.

God is raising men and women with the heart and revelation of the Father out there, into whose hands He shall place you and they shall, like the daughter of Pharaoh did with Moses when she called Moses' mother, raise you up for God. Nevertheless, the process of your coming out begins now.

The time you can't take it any more, that is the time to respond. The time the revelation controls you, that is the time to respond.

"Let My son go that he may serve Me."

God's call for His sons is clear. This is the time, the time of revelation. The time you hear this message, that is the time to come out in response. The time this truth and revelation comes to and catches you, that is the time to step out and step into placement as a son. Do not be ignorant but understand the time. It is the time to come out of 'Egypt'.

Hear the voice of the Son calling His sons from 'Egypt'. Today is the day of sonship to you. While you are waiting on God to work out the physical and practical arrangement, you need to respond now spiritually and rise from 'Egypt' by faith and action and step out into spiritual freedom.

- *Revelation of the Father*

> "And it came to pass when they were gone over, that Elijah said unto Elisha, Ask what I shall do for thee before I be taken from thee. And Elisha said, I pray thee, let a double portion of thy spirit be upon me. And he said,

> Thou hast asked a hard thing: nevertheless,
> if thou see me when I am taken from thee, it
> shall be so unto thee; but if not, it shall not be
> so . . . . And Elisha saw it, and he cried, My
> father, my father, the chariot of Israel, and
> the horsemen thereof. And he saw him no
> more . . ."
>
> 2 Kings 2:9-12

The whole time Elisha walked with Elijah, he knew that his master would be taken from his head. He was a servant under a master. At the time of reckoning, Elijah gives him a chance to ask for anything. What he asked for—the spirit—was connected with a revelation; the revelation of the Father. Because, as we shall later see, it is only the father who can give his spirit, and that also, can only be to his sons.

Elisha, while still hanging along as a faithful servant, begins to sense a swift transition in time that he lives in. Spiritual grounds are shifting under his prophetic feet by the new word Elijah gives him of "Ask," but he still lacks the revelation of the Father. His assignment is clearly cut out: He has to see beyond Elijah his master and catch the glimpse of God his Father. He has to see to receive sonship or else, he shall forever be bound in 'Egypt', serving but never fulfilled. The operative divine philosophy here is, 'you have to see the kingdom of God to enter the kingdom of God.'

You cannot be what you cannot see. Then Elisha saw it! He saw it, not him. He saw the very revelation that Elijah spoke of. He caught the revelation of the Father and this revelation was so overwhelmingly consuming and deeply life transforming that he could not hold himself. He burst out in deep, powerful and hearty declaration of revelation:

"My father, my father, . . ."

He saw the father! He saw the Father of heaven and earth, embodied in the person of Elijah. When he saw the Father, the servant mind could not stand anymore any longer. It just got renewed. What a revelation! The revelation of the Father is what makes a son. The renewal of his mind totally changed him and the man stepped into his place ordained for him right before the foundation of the world; the place of sonship. Sons are those who have the revelation and relationship with the Father. When the Father is not in view, the son is out of sight.

Most of the church today is languishing in 'Egypt', burdened with ministry and goals to accomplish because we have learned so much about the *Lord* and not about the *Father*. But when God is best known to us as *our Lord*, we can only be *His servants and slaves* at our best.

When the revelation of the Father comes, which is a key aspect of apostolic restoration today, the church will start to come forth out of bondage of 'Egypt' and step into sonship. It takes revelation of the Father to come out of 'Egypt'. Knowing Him as Father is key to changing our values from loving 'Egypt' to loving the promise.

Jesus as a Son, came into this world to reveal the Father.

> "No man hath seen God at any time: the only begotten Son, which is in the bosom of the Father, he hath declared him."
>
> John 1:18

Jesus came into the world to declare the Father. He is the revelation of the invisible God. As He declared Him in His speech and in His person, the world got to see the invisible

God. As we come to see Him, we get to know the Father, for He is the visible of the invisible God; what is seen of the God who cannot be seen.

> "Philip saith unto him, Lord show us the Father, and it sufficeth us. Jesus saith unto him, Have I been so long time with you, and yet hast thou not known me, Philip? He that hath seen Me hath seen the Father; and how sayest thou then, Show us the Father?"
>
> John 14:8-9

Philip was asking the revelation of the Father to reveal to him the Father, or better, he was asking the Father to show him the Father! Philip, like many other religious people, did not believe that the Son of God is the exact revelation of God, that the Father is revealed in the Son. Philip, like most of the church has done, was probably guilty of relegating the Son to the place of 'the second person in the Godhead'. Jesus is the exact revelation and representation of the invisible God. He is the visible of the invisible God. He is the eternal God come in the flesh of men; God housed in a body.

As the church gets to know Jesus as the Father, the church will be delivered from 'Egypt' to come to inheritance. The revelation of the Father is in His Son.

> "And the Word was made flesh, and dwelt among us, (and we beheld His glory, the glory as of the only begotten of the Father,) full of grace and truth"
>
> John 1:14

Christ is that which the first apostles heard (the Eternal Word), and saw (became flesh) and handled(became authentic in proof when they fellowshipped with Him).

Christ is the revelation of the glory, the fullness of the Father. Men saw God walking the earth in the body of Jesus. This is the mystery of godliness, that God was manifested in the flesh; not, the son of God was manifested in the flesh. 1 Tim 3:16

The Father is known by revelation. We need the spirit of wisdom and revelation in the knowledge of Him to come upon us daily that we may know Him and come to the excellency of the knowledge of Christ. The Father is revealed in His Son whom He sent to manifest Him.

So, Elisha saw the revelation of the Father and cried out, "My father, my father." And Christ is the revelation of the Father. So whom did Elisha see? He saw Christ. This suggests strongly that Elijah revealed the heavenly Father to him, and, when the revelation of the Father was in place, the servant got overhauled and stepped into sonship.

The Two Comings Of Elijah

The Book of Malachi concludes in this wise:

> "Behold, I will send you Elijah before the coming of the great and dreadful day of the LORD; and he shall turn the heart of the fathers to the children, and the heart of the children to their fathers, lest I come and smite the earth with a curse."
>
> Mal 4:5-6

There are a number of key insights that we need to glean in this high voltage passage;

One, there is something to *behold*. Any time the word 'behold' is used, an incredible revelation is coming forth, something unusual and weighty. We need to have the eyes of our understanding enlightened even as we receive the Spirit of wisdom and revelation in the knowledge of Him to behold this wonder. Are you ready?

Two, Elijah does not *just* come, he is *sent* by God. One who comes announces himself, introduces himself and does his will to draw attention to himself and gather people unto himself. This is the characteristic of modern day false prophets and apostles who come to create their niche in the societies of men. This Elijah is sent by God; God himself announces and introduces him and he reveals God who sent him and gathers attention and men unto the Sender; for he is an appointee of another. The word here is sent, which describes an apostle as a sent one, a messenger. This Elijah the prophet has immense apostolic properties.

Three, Elijah comes in a very *specific epoch*, in a chosen dispensation of time; he comes *before* the coming of the day of the LORD. This essentially implies that before there can be a great and awesome (dreadful) revelation of Christ, there must be first a sending and coming of Elijah. The revelation of the fullness of God in the earth is hence from thence tied to the precedential sending and coming of this Elijah. Therefore, whenever he comes, the world needs to see the coming of the Lord written on all the walls.

Four, Elijah comes for a very *specific purpose* and ministry; to turn in fathers primarily and to turn in sons secondarily. The father comes before the son. Like we had said above, the revelation of the Father is what restores the son into his place. Home is defined from the father's point of view, not the son's.

The purpose of Elijah's coming

Elijah comes to bring out and bring up the Father, then as a consequence, to bring out and bring up the sons.

He comes to reveal the Father in the house then bring the sons home. He comes to heal the family of God. He carries the revelation of the Father who sends him and he adequately reveals Him in such a way that sons come into their placement.

He comes essentially to repair the Father's tent which was broken down; to build the house of the Father so Father and son can once again get together and commune as one.

He comes for sons; to bring them to their place of elevated relationship with the Father.

This is the ministry and purpose of Elijah.

Five, the sending and coming of Elijah is *the last line of defense against divine curse upon the earth*. God's word is clear, "lest I smite the earth with a curse."

We all know this too well; when the first son was lost in the Garden of Eden, God smote the earth with the curse sweat, thorns, thistles, etc.

Sonship is the divine design; the absence of it is recipe for a divine curse.

In the Old Testament, God raised and sent Elijah to reveal Him in His nation, Israel. He was a spiritual father. He was raised at a time when the whole nation had largely fallen from the Father's house and was communing with other gods, the Baals and the Asherah. The priesthood had lost the father's heart and mandate and led God's people into idol temples and worship. Elijah's mission was to reveal the Father and His divine design and to turn the heart of the nation back to the Father.

His heartfelt prayer on the top of Mount Carmel best reveals in summary this mission and ministry that God sent him into;

> "LORD God of Abraham, Isaac and Israel, let it be known this day that thou art God in Israel . . . . Hear me, O LORD, hear me that this people may know that thou art the LORD God, and that thou hast turned their hearts back again."
>
> 1Kings 18:36, 37.

His ministry was to reveal the Father God and to turn back sons to the Father.

After the Lord's transfiguration on the mount, the disciples raised with Him the question of the coming of Elijah. Jesus' answer pointed at two dispensations of Elijah, depicted in the two different tenses He employed.

> "And His disciples asked Him, saying, 'Why then do the scribes say that Elijah must come first?' Jesus answered and said to them, 'Indeed Elijah is coming first and will restore all things. But I say to you that Elijah has come already, and they did not know him but did to him whatever they wished. Likewise the Son of Man is also about to suffer at their hands.' Then the disciples understood that He spoke to them about John the Baptist."
>
> Matt 17:10-13.

Jesus' answer puts the coming of Elijah into two contexts; present and future. He says, "Elijah is coming and will restore all things." Then he says, "Elijah has come." The future coming is connected to the restoration of all things. It's more comprehensive and demanding. The present coming doesn't bear that allusion but we know the purpose and ministry of Elijah. The present coming of Elijah (at the time Jesus made this statement) was fulfilled in John the Baptist. John the Baptist came into this world as Elijah; not in Elijah's flesh and blood but in his spirit and power;

> "to turn the hearts of fathers to the children and to turn the disobedient to the wisdom of the just. To make ready a people prepared for the Lord."
>
> Luke 1:17 (nkjv)

John the Baptist came before the first coming of the Lord and he prepared the people for the Lord by calling the backslidden sons of God to repentance and faith toward God. He came to reveal the Father who was about to fully come into the earth embodied in human flesh, the man Christ Jesus. John's ministry never drew people unto himself but pointed at and revealed Christ, our Everlasting Father. As a matter of fact, the more John taught and talked, the more he lost disciples. Whomsoever he lost, Jesus found, and for all this he had the spirit and power of Elijah to thank. What a great apostolic type he was!

However great that was, there remained another coming of the Lord, another great and dreadful (judgment) day of the Lord and by consequence, another sending of Elijah remained. Beyond John the Baptist, Jesus expanded our expectations and said, "Elijah is coming and will restore all things". The best coming of Elijah was reserved for the consummation of all things that God spoke by the mouth of all His holy prophets since the world began (Acts 3:19-21).

We are living in such an awesome and specific epoch, in such a clearly prophetic dispensation of time, in which Elijah is sent again; not in flesh and blood, but as was with John, in spirit and power; to destroy the curse and prepare the earth for a blessing by revealing the Father and turning in sons.

There is a quick work going on in the earth through the spirit and power of Elijah today. The restoration of all things is rapidly and steadily on going even in the face of all the ugliness and fears the world faces today. Recently on our way to Nairobi and in the company of Dr Jim Lindsey and Pastor Ibrahim, I was driving through a terrible section of the Kisumu-Nakuru highway. That section of the road was a nightmare and to make matters even worse, we drove in the night. Most of that section of the road was ploughed out to prepare for fresh carpeting and expansion of the road. By the time we got to the Eldoret-Nakuru highway, my car was falling apart; the wheels were wobbling, the brakes were slipping and the CV joints were really rattling. The road looked very ugly. Yes, they made it ugly first before they could make it beautiful.

In the restoration process, things can and do get pretty ugly, rough, tough and uncomfortable before they get beautiful. Some of the ugly things we face today and the world leaders complain of could be the process of restoration, "of making the road better and broader". The true holy apostles and prophets of Christ are essentially instrumental and Christ's deeper revelation is undoubtedly central in all this. What we have hitherto known as church must be substantially and dimensionally adjusted to appreciate all this magnanimous undertaking in this chosen hour.

To prepare the earth for His first individual coming, Elijah was sent in the individual body of John the Baptist. However, now, to prepare the earth and world for His ultimate second coming, and taking comprehensive cognizance of the magnanimity of the task—the restoration of all things before the Lord comes—even in this our blessed time, Elijah has been sent in a corporate Body called Apostles, Prophets, Evangelists, Pastors and Teachers, and specifically leading this team are apostles. These are the days of Elijah!

Why do I say that the present day Elijah is a corporate body and is personified in the apostles? For starters, the first coming of Christ was in an individual body that walked the earth as one man. However this time, he is coming in His fullness, the Head and His Body, made perfect in one and manifesting One God in the earth. It took an individual to prepare the earth for an individual appearance of the Lord. It is going to take a corporate body to prepare the earth for a corporate appearance and manifestation of the corporate Christ; the perfect man, the man and His wife, the Head and His body. His body is going to be fully and perfectly found in Him, having grown and come to the measure of the stature of the fullness of Christ.

Why is this great movement apostolic? Because apostles are sent ones, sent by God, to reveal the Father thereby raise many sons unto God, and to build His house (family) as the wise master builders put in charge and oversight(1 Cor 3:9-11). This end-time Elijah is not a person, but a movement; a spiritual unstoppable movement led by apostles and prophets; a movement of saints who come into the revelation of the Father and walk as sons of God in the earth. Whoever sees this movement shall cry out, "My Father! My Father!" because this movement reveals

Christ, our Everlasting Father and Christ is the revelation and manifestation of the invisible God.

Whoever sees Christ cries out, My Father! No one has ever seen the Father at any time. The only begotten Son, who is at the bosom of the Father, He has manifested Him.

> "For He is the image of the invisible God; the firstborn over all creation"
>
> Col 1:15

He is the invisible God manifested in the flesh of mortal men.

What a glorious revelation Elisha had! How did he know it was Christ? By revelation. Christ can only be known by revelation.

> "But when it pleased God, who separated me from my mother's womb and called me through His grace, to reveal His Son in me that I might preach Him among the Gentiles, I did not confer with flesh and blood . . ."
>
> Gal 1:15-16

No flesh and blood told Paul on the way to Damascus that He who spoke with him was the Lord, yet he screamed,

> "Who art thou, Lord?"
>
> Acts 9:5

> "But this shall be the covenant that I will make with the house of Israel; after those days, saith the LORD, I will put my law in their inward parts, and write it in their hearts; and will be their God and they shall be my people.

> And they shall teach no more every man his
> neighbor, and every man his brother saying,
> Know the LORD: for they shall all know me,
> from the least of them unto the greatest of
> them ..."
>
> Jer 31:33-34

We are the children of the new covenant; a covenant
written in our hearts and put in our minds; a covenant of
the Spirit taught by the Spirit; a covenant whose centrality
and consistency is the revelation of the Father.

So, both Elisha and Saul of Tarsus knew Him without
someone teaching them. They received revelation from
the Spirit. The same was the case with Simon when Jesus
asked, 'Who do you say that I the Son of Man, am?'

The Father is known and seen by revelation.

The Father is seen in Jesus.

The Father is seen as the Christ.

The Father is seen in the Son.

- *The Spirit Of Sonship*

> "And Jesus, when he was baptized, went
> up straightaway out of the water: and lo, the
> heavens were opened unto him, and he saw
> the Spirit of God descending like a dove, and
> lighting upon him: And lo, a voice from heaven
> saying, This is my beloved Son, in whom I am
> well-pleased."
>
> Matt 3:16-17

It was after the Spirit rested on Him that the voice identified Him as the Son. Of course we know that Jesus is the eternal Son of God: but for the purposes of manifesting to men the pattern, the divine design, this occurred at His baptism. This was not just an anointing or a power; it was the Spirit that identifies and places sons of God; the Spirit of sonship.

The descent and entrance of the Spirit into His life delivered Him from the order of the Old Testament levitical priesthood, and conveyed Him into a new order; the order of Melchizedeck. This is the order of God's sons. He received the Spirit of the Father that identified Him with the Father as a Son. We must receive this Spirit for us to come out of the old system of Egyptian slavery, into our new dimension.

> "For ye have not received the spirit of bondage again to fear; but ye have received the spirit of adoption, whereby we cry, Abba, Father."
>
> Rom 8:15

> "And because ye are sons, God hath sent forth the Spirit of his Son into your hearts, crying, Abba, Father."
>
> Gal 4:6

> "For as many as are led by the Spirit of God they are the sons of God."
>
> Rom 8:14

You need the Spirit of sonship in order to come out of bondage to fear. He is the Spirit that portrays the perfect love of the Father which casts out all fear. This is the spirit who shall change you from within; a transformation from servant hood to sonship; an inner change of person, heart, attitude and focus.

So here we have the pattern;

God creates Adam and breathes into him the breath of the spirit of life; this makes him a son.

God pours upon Jesus the Spirit at His baptism; this makes Him a Son.

Jesus pours His Spirit to the disciples and apostles on the day of Pentecost; this makes them sons.

Elijah gives Elisha his spirit; this makes him a son.

- *Faith*

> "By faith he forsook Egypt; not fearing the wrath of the King: for he endured, as seeing him who is invisible."
>
> Heb 11:27

> "Have faith in God."
>
> Mark 11:22

> "Now faith is the substance of the things hoped for, the evidence of the things not seen."
>
> Heb 11:1

It took faith for Moses to stand up against all the luxuries that surrounded him in Egypt, and accept suffering with the children of God in faith that God shall bring them to the land of promise, the dimension of fulfillment; a land flowing with milk and honey.

He had faith and absolute trust in God, not wavering in faith but trusting that He who promised is faithful and shall fulfill His word.

If we are willing to truly turn away from 'Egypt', we must be willing to absolutely repent from the dead works of 'Egypt' in order for us to have unalloyed faith in God. Without this quality of faith we will always be looking back to 'Egypt' as we move on.

Faith never looks back, but ever looks forward. It expects to see what it believes. Faith is the spiritual transportation of tomorrow into today, into now. Faith is the declaration of the end from the beginning; the celebration before the event.

God says 'no looking back as you move. Sodom is coming under judgment because it killed the witnesses and crucified the Lord. Lot, no looking back as you move forward, or you get disqualified.'

> "But his wife looked back from behind him,
> and she became a pillar of salt."
>
> Gen 19:26

Her heart lusted for Sodom and her lustful eyes strayed back casually but romantically as her lips blew a flying kiss to the pagan idols of Sodom and Gomorrah. This was too much and the Lord, whose name is Jealous, would have none of it. He took her out. She had failed the kingdom suitability test.

Jesus makes it very crystal:

> ". . . No man having put his hands to the
> plow, and looking back, is fit for the kingdom
> of God."
>
> Luke 9:62

To overcome the world and its lusts, we must have the victory that overcomes the world.

> ". . . and this is the victory that overcometh
> the world, even our faith."
>
> 1 John 5:4

By faith we shall break loose from the vicious tentacles of 'Egypt' and stand on a new ground; the ground of our definition in Christ as sons of God.
It will require strong and unwavering faith to deny 'Egypt' and walk out to the invisible.

Weighing the promises of Pharaoh in Egypt, the food and how it made you full, on one hand, and now armed with revelation of your destiny, the word of faith and faith on the other hand, you get persuaded in your spirit, with nothing tangible to hang on, to walk out on 'Egypt'. This takes faith in God.
How much do you believe the word of the Lord concerning your destiny?

- *Decisiveness*

> "By faith Moses, when he was come to
> years, refused to be called the son of Pharaoh's
> daughter, choosing rather to suffer affliction
> with the people of God, than to enjoy the
> pleasures of sin for a season."
>
> Heb 11:24-26

Decision making is key to coming out of 'Egypt'. That is why when the Israelites left Egypt, there were even some Egyptians who left with them. They decided to leave too. However, most of the time the Israelites encountered harsh conditions, they sought to return to Egypt. That was a sign of mental weakness. They could not decide and pay the price of their decisions. This is not an easy decision. It is a costly one and one has to be willing to pay the full price to come out of 'Egypt'.

Moses considered his options, calculated the cost of rejecting Egypt and got up. Egypt offered him food, security, women, chariots, luxury, education, a reputation, a fat pay cheque, name it. He rode on royal chariots and had whatever he wanted. Egypt made him full. Was he going to deny all that for the sake of his relentless pursuit for fulfillment? Was he going to throw away through the window all that which came on a silver platter for the sake of fulfillment that will cause him pain in the process? He was full, yes, but he was unfulfilled. He weighed the two and made up his mind. It was time to suffer in the will of God than enjoy in the place of doom. He was willing to lay it all down for the excellency of the promise.

Apostle Paul says,

> "But what things were gain to me, those I counted loss for Christ. Yea doubtless, and I count all things but loss for the excellency of the knowledge of Christ Jesus my Lord: for whom I have suffered the loss of all things, and do count them but dung, that I may win Christ."
>
> Phil 3:7-8

This is decision making. This is decisiveness. He was willing to lose all things that he might excel in knowing Christ. The revelation of Christ was more important to him than anything else. No one is going to be pulled out of 'Egypt'. Each one must be willing enough to obey the voice of the Father and come out. That is why the revelation of the Father is key.

No one told Simon Peter at the lake Gennesaret to forsake his trade. The very fish he toiled the whole night to catch, he forsook and all at the shore and followed Jesus.

> "So when they had brought their boats to land, they forsook all and followed Him."
> Luke 5:11. (nkjv)

He did this because in Christ he saw the fulfillment of his life, the fullness.

When the prodigal son remembered home and his father, he willingly got up and started home. It was a conscious and deliberate decision he made or else, he would soon be back in the woods.

Have you made up your mind to come out of that system in spite of the abundance and goodness it offered you, and be obedient to the heavenly vision of the Father and your destiny? Do you seek to be full or fulfilled?

You cannot come out based on euphoria; you can't come out because your friends and neighbours are coming out and you don't want to miss them. This is a personal decision you have to make.

I remember when the apostolic was boiling hot in my womb and God was gracing me with grace and opening doors to the gift and grace. I was by then serving in a large Pentecostal church in my city, had an office, a pay package and was being transported in the ministry van every Sunday.

I was being paid twice; every Sunday after Service and every end of the month. We hade a good congregation, about 500 saints attending each Sunday and we had three services every Sunday. I was one of the associate pastors in that ministry.

Nevertheless, things just started going wrong. My relationship with my Bishop wasn't great because the apostolic calling was always interfering with my clearly cut, custom-tailored duties as a pastor. I was always needed to be around, to run the lunch hour meetings, bury the dead, preach in the services and be at the office counseling;precisely to be a good pastor.

This wasn't happening well and I was clearly letting that ministry down big time. I would be responding to apostolic missions to teach and train leaders in other towns and cities and my heart would always give this apostolic responsibility the first priority. Sooner than later, I was summoned to the office and was asked to choose between what my denomination expected me to do; be a good pastor and carry out my pastoral duties diligently and submissively, and leaving the ministry if I insisted in doing what was carrying me away.

I tried to explain that I really did not want to leave but simply wanted to be allowed to respond to the apostolic call upon my life fully while having that ministry as the base. This was not tolerated. I paused and thought. My wife was still at the hospital, having just put to bed our daughter Jannet. That meant I needed money to pay bills at the hospital. It was end of the month and so all the bills were due including rent. We needed food too and some warm clothes for the new baby.

How was I going to throw away in one afternoon something I had really depended on and I had no other visible means of income? My bishop was waiting. One of the pastors had been brought in as a witness. I cleared my voice and said something like this;

"Well, I guess I will have to be obedient to the heavenly vision and continue with the apostolic work."

That brought the curtain on my service and tenure with that denomination—and on all the benefits and privileges that came with it—and marked the beginning of a very difficult time in my life.

I think and still shudder at the very thought of all I went through. I think that that was one of the most difficult and fiery times I have ever undergone in my life—considering that I was barely a year old in marriage and had a few days' old baby to look after without money coming from anywhere. That was tough but that was a decision I was and still am glad I did make. God did come through after some dry and consuming months and my situation began to change, for the better.

Today, I am most grateful to God I made the decision I did. My soul and destiny were set free and I began to fly toward my inheritance as a son. Though I am not always full, I have awesome fulfillment and great peace in my life. I have travelled more and been to several nations taking the apostolic message. I have learned from what I went through to be a better man and minister and a father to those with and under me.

I have grown in the word and love for my Bible deeply. I have conducted great apostolic gatherings and raised sons all over Kenya, into Tanzania, Burundi, DR Congo, Islamic

Republic of Pakistan, Bahrain, Cyprus, USA, South Africa, just to mention but a few. I have seen the faithfulness and the provision of the Lord too in my life.

Today, at the writing of this book, my daughter Jannet is full of life, vibrant and celebrates her ninth birthday. What more can a man ask for?

All these things the Lord had room to accomplish in my life because I dared to come out of a system that hadn't been prepared at that time to nurture and nurse the apostolic and I decided to offer myself to Him as an offering in my wilderness. I am aware that so much good has happened in that ministry today, and I am glad.

I thank all those God used, especially Apostle Paul Galligan of Revival Ministries Australia, to aid me through the process and help me find my apostolic feet in due time. Your encouragement and fathering made me what I am today and the best is yet to come.

> "By faith Abraham, when he was called to go out into a place which he should after receive for an inheritance, obeyed; and he went out not knowing whither he went."
>
> Heb 11:8

This is the kind of decision we must make; a decision to move from the familiar to the unfamiliar; from the comfortable to the uncomfortable.

It has to be a decision of faith and revelation. It is a decision you make when you say, 'I have had enough of this 'Egypt' thing and I am better off without it. I am willing to obey God and be obedient to the voice of the Father calling me out. I want out and I want out now!'

If one is still toying with Egyptian dolls, it is not possible for such a one to make this decision to leave 'Egypt'. All the time Abraham toyed around with Lot, he could not let go. Infact when God allowed circumstances to divorce Lot from his life, he marshaled an army and went for Lot and brought him back to his life. While you are still sympathetic and sentimental about 'Egypt', you cannot crucify it.

I know of those wonderful brethren whom the Lord called into ministry but could not imagine a life without their pay cheque. So they began to make great savings before they would obey God; just to have some cushion for safe landing when the worst happens in the wilderness of ministry. The wisdom of God in responding to ministry call dictates that the sending of the Lord and His timing are more important than our own protection mechanisms.

Twice Jesus sent His disciples and twice He sent them differently. At one time, He sent them *without*, and at another, He sent them *with*. At both times, they lacked nothing in the process and the end.

> ". . . When I sent you without purse, and scrip, and shoes, lacked ye anything? And they said, Nothing. Then he said unto them, But now, he that hath a purse, let him take it, and likewise his scrip: and he that hath no sword, let him sell his garment and buy one."
>
> Luke 22:35-36

- *A Redeemer*

> "And the Redeemer shall come to Zion, and unto them that turn from transgression in Jacob, saith the LORD."
>
> Isa 59:20

> "Come now therefore, and I will send thee unto Pharaoh, that thou mayest bring forth my people the children of Israel from Egypt."
>
> Ex 3:10

> "Peter therefore was kept in prison . . . . And behold, the angel of the Lord came upon him, and a light shined in prison: and he smote Peter on the side, and raised him up, saying, Arise up quickly. And his chains fell off from his hands . . ."
>
> Acts 12:5-7

To come out of 'Egypt', one greater than the prisoner must be sent into the prison; one who has what it takes to break into the bondage system and deliver the sons, will have to be sent.

God took time with Moses, preparing him for forty years before he was ready as a deliverer to be sent back into Egypt to deliver the sons of God. Those who obeyed his voice and command were delivered with a great and mighty arm and carried on eagle's wings through the wilderness to the inheritance.

God is sending a Redeemer into Zion. Zion should, normally, be the place where deliverers are sent from to go forth into the world and deliver sons. However, in this case, the opposite is true. Zion has become very religious; bearing a godly name but dead in traditions and ways of men and fallen into sin and iniquity. This is the state of most of what is called church today.

Sons of God are perishing in the 'church' and a redeemer has to be sent.

God is taking time today and raising apostles whom He is sending to the church today to redeem His sons from 'Egypt' and bring them to their inheritance. A lot of resistance the apostolic ministry is experiencing today in the contemporary church is from the 'Pharaohs' who are lords over God's people and feel they own the people.

They are not willing to receive the apostles because they know when they do, great light will shine in their prisons—sorry, churches—and the sons of God shall be brought out, like the angel did to Peter. Angels are ministers of God, and many times the word "angel" does refer to human messengers sent by God to accomplish a great task.

The church is in prayer and believes God needs to 'visit' the Church with a 'revival'. God is already answering their prayer—His own way. He is sending apostolic angels, angels called apostles, to His Zion which has become a prison, an 'Egypt', where His sons are bound and held awaiting execution; like they killed the two witnesses.

Apostles are already coming. If they have not reached your ministry and church, dear pastor, dear Bishop, know they are at the door. They are sent by God to redeem His sons; to bring the revelation of Christ to the body so the saints can quickly see the Father and grow up into maturity, ready to step out in order to step into their placements. The redeemers are coming, armed with the grace, authority, humility, character, word and revelation of Christ to bring to His sons.

When the apostolic ministry is received, Christ is received; and when Christ is received, the Father who sent Him is received (Matt 10:40) So if the Father is in Christ and Christ is fully revealed to His apostles, then it goes without saying that when we receive the apostles whom He sends to us, we receive the fullness of God embodied in them.

Times have changed; God is not only looking for servants who can serve Him well, He is looking for sons who shall serve His purpose and be led of His Spirit. The covering of Christ is coming upon His church through the apostles He is sending. This is because apostles are non-denominational; they have no denomination of their own to propagate; they do not reveal who they are but who sent them; they are commissioners of Christ and come in the name of the Lord.

Jesus, as an apostle of our confession, explains how apostles come while referring to Himself;

> "If any man will do his will, he shall know of the doctrine, whether it be of God, or whether I speak of myself. He that speaketh of himself seeketh his own glory: but he that seeketh his glory that sent him, the same is true, and no unrighteousness is in him."
>
> John 7:17-18

> "Then cried Jesus in the temple as he taught, saying, Ye both know me, and ye know whence I am: and I am not come of myself, but he that sent me is true, whom ye know not. But I know him: for I am from him, and he hath sent me."
>
> John 7:28-29

Apostles do not come to start branches of their ministries and churches in your city but rather, to work with you in your city, in all humility, labouring day and night with tears to see Christ formed in every city, village, township and nation; to see the corporate Elijah body arise; to see the body of sons emerge in the earth, ready for planting in the world. Apostles do not come to take the place of Bishops or pastors or prophets. They come to set all these in order so that grace can be released to the body for edification.

It is time to receive the apostles for they are being sent as redeemers to deliver and raise sons unto God, not unto themselves. I thank the people who were willing to play this role in my life. They came as redeemers in our Zion.

The angel that came into Peter's prison cell was an apostolic angel; a messenger sent from Christ with the word and authority of Christ to deliver the apostle from Egyptian bondage. There are many today who are called into apostolic ministry but their churches or denominations do not believe in apostles functioning today, or do not know who apostles are and so they cannot identify the gifting in order to develop it for glorious display and functioning. Many frustrated pastors today and hopeless teachers may simply be apostles in the rough; confined in religious coffins awaiting a burial service, stuck in strange molds and unable to joyfully serve.

When angel apostles come, they shall by the grace and revelation they carry be able to ignite these gifts and identify them and raise them up. The light that shone in the cell where Peter was, was a type of the revelation of Christ that apostles carry. This is the truth of the pure word, apostles' doctrine. This is the truth that when revealed and we get to know, we are set free.

> "And ye shall know the truth and the truth shall set ye free."
>
> John8:32

There is a light that shines when true apostles come, are received and minister. The mystery of God in the Bible gets revealed, clarity comes, eyes of understanding get opened and lives get transformed. This is the glowing glory of His person being revealed through their message and grace, and men can behold it; notice it and have fellowship with it: and it is full of grace and truth. True apostolic ministry cannot leave a town the same; cannot leave lives the same, when it is well received. A lot of skepticism and resistance to the apostolic has limited apostolic manifestation in great grace and authority and the church has largely remained desolate all this while; head stuck in the traditions of men.

> "O Jerusalem, Jerusalem, thou that killest the prophets, and stonest them which are sent unto thee, how often would I have gathered thy children together, even as a hen gathereth her chickens under her wings, and ye would not! Behold your house is left unto you desolate. For I say unto you, Ye shall not see me henceforth, till ye shall say, Blessed is he that cometh in the name of the Lord."
>
> Matt 23:37-39.

In this context, Jerusalem, God's house of peace, is guilty of two crimes;
One, it killed the prophets (those who spoke against her evil practices and called her to repentance), two, it stoned those sent to her (apostles who came to restore it). Jerusalem killed the prophets and stoned the apostles—the two key ministries given the revelation of the mystery of Christ in unequaled measure.(Eph 3:2-5). When these two gifts are resisted, Christ's deep revelation and grace for maturity is stumbled and kept away.

Redeemers are coming and we are grateful to God for them. When apostles and prophets come, they come as sons to save God's house from destruction and illegal occupancy. We shall see more of this later in this book in the last chapter, "Showing the house to the house"

• *The Passover Lamb*

> "Your lamb shall be without blemish, a male of the first year: ye shall take it out from the sheep, or from the goats: and ye shall keep it up until the fourteenth day of the same month: and the whole assembly of the congregation of Israel shall kill it in the evening . . . . And the blood shall be to you for a token upon the houses where you are: and when I see the blood, I will pass over you . . ."
>
> Ex 12:5, 6, 13

> "The next day, John seeth Jesus coming unto him, and saith, Behold, the Lamb of God, which taketh away the sin of the world."
>
> John 1:29

> "In whom we have redemption through his blood, even the forgiveness of sins:"
>
> Col 1:14

Jesus came into the world with an offering that was stronger than death and the bondage thereof. He came into this world with His blood to redeem all those who shall put their trust and faith in Him. He is the acceptable, pure, qualified Lamb of God without blemish whom God used in type in Egypt to deliver the firstborn out of Egypt. His offering delivers us from all existence and appearance of

'Egypt'. By His blood, we are redeemed from the shackles of 'Egypt'.

- *The Son*

> "For God so loved the world that He gave His only begotten Son, that whoever believes in Him should not perish but have everlasting life."
>
> John 3:16

God lost a son in the garden of Eden. He sent His Son to seek and save His lost son's sons. It takes a son to find a son and redeem a son. Like the English proverb says, 'Set a thief to catch a thief', God sent His son to catch sons.

Jesus came into the world as the pattern Son of the Father, the Darling of the Father, so that all prospective sons would see and know what they are being called into. He is an admirable Son, a son anybody would like to ape.

As many as received the pattern Son, the same gave them power to become sons of God. The Son came to reproduce Himself in multitudes of sons in those who receive Him.

> "For you are all sons of God through faith in Christ Jesus."
>
> Gal 3:26

Knowing the Son and relating with the Son delivers us from perishing in the outer worlds where Adam and his wife were cast, and restores us to eternal life in the Father's garden.

> "Christ has redeemed us from the curse of the law, having become a curse for us (for it is

written, 'Cursed is everyone who hangs on a
tree).'"

Gal 3:13

Christ is the Son of God. The Son came and hung on a
tree for our redemption. Only the price of a Son would
the Father accept for the redemption of His sons. Behold
what manner of love the Father has bestowed upon us, that
we, who were lost and dead in 'Egypt', should be delivered
by the offering of His only begotten Son; that we should
become and be called sons unto God! Thank you the Son
for making me a son.

- *The Rhema Word*

Joseph was told to "stay in Egypt until I bring you word."
So much time has gone by and all this while, you have
been in 'Egypt'. Yes, you have been waiting for the Lord
to bring you word. The word has now come to you in your
Egyptian system. His word comes with His messenger, His
angel. The seasons have changed. The time of 'Egypt' is up
and now hear the call:

> "Arise, take the young Child and his mother
> and go into the land of Israel: for they are dead
> which sought the young child's life."

Matt 2:20.

The word coming to you is, Arise. The angel who came to
Peter in prison said to him, Arise. To cross over the Jordan
and step into the land of promise, God's word to Joshua
was, Arise. It is time to arise from the place of bondage,
where you are always serving and never being fulfilled.
The word of the Lord to the man who sat in the porches
by the pool for thirty eight years, was, Arise. The word
of Christ to His church that has sat in the porches of

denominationalism and legalism and error is, Arise! It is time to come out of darkness into His marvelous light. It is time to decamp from the children of darkness into the sons of light camp.

> "Arise, shine; for thy light is come, and the
> glory of the LORD is risen upon thee."
>
> Isa 60:1

It is time for sons of God to come out of Egypt, to enter into their placement and inherit all things.

CHAPTER THREE

The Reasons For Sons

While I have been able to share much on this, it is worth taking a more close look and discernment of the heart of the Father. God is so consumed with the issue of sonship. He is 'desperate' for sons, in the sense that He is ready at home and waiting for sons to be through with their prodigy, pick up them selves from 'Egypt' and come home. His arms are wide open. It is time to come home. Why is this? Why is the Father so passionate about sons?

Before we fully discuss this, it is important at this point to point out that this teaching on sonship refers to the mature ones in the Father; those who have come to know the Father and are well-pleasing unto Him.

Well, below are some of the reasons why sons of God are needed by the Father:

- *Sons bear the image of the Father*

When God created the first son, He created him in His own image. It was God's plan right from the beginning to have Himself revealed in the earth through an entity. This chosen entity is sons of God. The Father is seen in the Son and so by having many sons in the earth, can you imagine the abundance of the revelation of the Father that the earth would have to deal with?

The revelation of the Father is in the son. The sons are the visible of the invisible Father. The Father wants to be known in the earth. There is no way the Father would have been known in a more personal way, if Jesus would not have come into the world. He came as the Son of God to reveal God to men and to all creation by extension. This Son left the earth having set in motion the dynamics that work to raise many sons unto God in the earth.

By seeing sons of God, the Father is revealed to all men and creation again. God is not a secret any more. His sons reveal Him and make Him known.

Jesus said, 'He that has seen Me has seen the Father'.
Son of God is equal to God manifested in the flesh. Jesus as a Son was and is the Father's equal. The Jews wanted to stone Jesus for two great reasons; one, He healed a man on a Sabbath and even commanded him to carry his bed on that holy day. Two, He, being a man, called God His Father thereby "making Himself equal with God" John 5:18. The Jews of His day knew that to say 'son of' is the same as saying 'equal of'.

God wants to raise sons in the earth who are His equal, that is, who shall fully and correctly reveal and represent Him in the earth. The goal of the five ministry gifts is to ensure that we grow until we come to 'the measure of the stature of the fullness of Christ." Eph 4:13

This brings us to His level, whereby whoever looks at us and looks at Him sees one and the same thing. God shall be seen in the earth fully revealed in His sons. Men and women shall look at the mature sons of God, in the earth, revealing the Christ; doing the works of the Christ, only speaking the words of Christ, walking fully in the ways of Christ, and they shall say, "Behold the Christ of God!"

The prodigal son, upon returning home, was dressed with and in the father's robe. That completely baptized him in the father. Whoever saw him saw the father. This is the plan of the Father.

> "Those whom He foreknew, He also predestined to be conformed into the image of His Son that He might be the firstborn among many brethren."
>
> Rom 8:29

Sons bear the image of and hence reveal the Father.

- *Sons house the father*

Sons are the preferred residence of the father. At the baptism of Jesus, the voice from heaven said,
This is My Beloved Son, IN WHOM I AM well pleased.

The Father publically declared to all creation that from that time hence forth, whoever shall be looking for the Father, shall have to find Him in His Son, well pleased.

Where is the Father? In His Son. How is He there? Well pleased.

As sons of God come out of Egypt, the Father is increasing His residence in the earth among men, among His sons.

The Father desired to dwell in His people but they were still in Egypt. He came through His son and called them out. The Father has been looking for residence among men and this residence is called sons of God.

> "It pleased the Father that in Him should all the fullness dwell."
>
> Col 1:19

The fullness of the Father, all that make the Father the Father, dwelt in Christ His Son. The son comes in the fullness of the revelation of the Father. Sons of God discuss the Father; not ministries and work. It is servants who discuss work and talk about their pay and how much they earned last time.

Sons are full of the Father and when they open their mouths, it is a Father talk. So to listen to the Son is like listening to the Father. The Father dwells in His sons. As sons of God increase and mature and manifest in the earth, God shall be more abundantly found and accessed in the earth.

This is God's goal.

- *Sons receive the Spirit of the Father without measure*

It is the Spirit of the Father that identifies the son. Those whom the Father has called into sonship, He pours out on them the Spirit of adoption. This Spirit without measure is to give the sons unlimited access to the Father and also to lead them as they walk in their inheritance.

> "And because you are sons, God hath sent forth the Spirit of his Son into your hearts, crying, Abba, Father."
>
> Gal 4:6

- *Sons are led by the Spirit.*

Sons are mature ones who know the will and the heart of the Father. They do not need rules and regulations in order to know what to do. They do not need neither are they kept under tutors(the law) and guardians but are free from the rudimentary elements of this life and are freely led by the Spirit of the Father into His will and good pleasure.

They are led by the Spirit, not the flesh, of the Father. The Spirit of the Father leads sons to the perfect will of the Father.

This is a level where self is not allowed. It is all His will, the will of the Father being done. So Jesus could say, 'what I hear My Father speak, that I speak in like manner; and what I see My Father do, that I do in like manner.'

> "For as many as are led by the Spirit of God,
> they are the sons of God."
>
> Rom 8:14

• *Sons access the mysteries of the Father*

Sons are representatives of the Father and are the ones who reveal Him. As such, all that the Father withholds from others, He will make known to His sons so that they may go out and accurately reveal and represent Him. Jesus said 'the Son who is in the bosom of the Father, He is the one who has revealed the Father'. One has to have access to the bosom for one to know the mysteries therein. The apostolic ministry brings great revelation of the mysteries of God because apostles come as sons, walking in humility and obedience to the Father. They have nothing personal to prove or achieve. It's all about Christ and His will that they live and/or die for.

> "For the Father loveth the Son, and showeth
> him all things that himself doeth: and he will
> show him greater works than these, that ye
> may marvel."
>
> John 5:20

From the time I received the message and revelation of sonship, and stood before the Father and asked Him to place me as a son and fill me with the Spirit of His Son that I might know Him and walk before Him as a son, my life never remained the same, ever. The next time I looked at the Bible, the revelation just began pouring into my soul and I could not hold back my tears. Even those passages that I had read before and never made any sense began to make much sense.

The word of God started streaming live into my heart from the spiritual sources. I could stand and teach for two hours without opening my Bible but correctly and accurately quoting the Scriptures. Some of my sons got amazed at me. I told them it was the same thing I had witnessed happening in my spiritual father, when I was on a trip with him to Central Africa and he would get up and preach and teach for hours without opening his Bible once yet quote over twenty verses correctly.
It is the access to the mysteries of God that sons have.

- *Sons have dominion over all creation*

The first sons God created He gave dominion over the whole earth. God's authority in heaven flows on earth through His sons. The authority that apostles have is the authority of sons, that is why a key reason for the restoration of apostles is the restoration of the revelation of the Father so that sons may be restored.

> ". . . and let them have dominion over the
> fish of the sea, and over the fowl of the air, and
> over the cattle, and over all the earth, . . ."
> Gen 1:26

Adam as a son had incredible dominion over the birds of the air, over the cattle on the land, over the fish in the water and over everything that moves on the face of the earth. The earth, the air and the waters are under the domain of sons of God. Jesus spoke to the winds and they obeyed Him and the people asked, who is this? The answer is, He is the Son of God. He walked on water, subdued a donkey that had never been trained, spoke to the fig tree and commanded demons. All these awesome things He did as a Son of God.

By mid 2012, we were set to host my dad at our ministry base in Kakamega. The dates he gave us coincided with a very rainy season and here in Kakamega when it begins to rain, it pours; being on a hill full of trees, and on the edge of Kakamega Forest. Two weeks to the two days of the seminar, it was pouring torrentially daily, day and night. In one of our Sunday services, I stood up and prayed that it shall not rain for the days of the seminar but only before and after. I am glad many heard it. It kept on pounding the earth until a day to the first day of the seminar. The day before the day of the seminar, it rained so heavily the dirt road to the venue was all muddy and slippery.

The first day of the seminar, we all woke up to a beautiful dry weather, with the sun warmly smiling over us, the whole day, and the night was dry too. So was day two. At the end of the gathering, I told one of our pastors who was closing the meeting to remember to release the rain, now that we had finished the meetings.

We did not get home that night. We finished the meetings by 4 pm and by 6 pm, dark heavy rain clouds all of sudden gathered over us and hung low. Before night fall, it rained so heavily as if to redeem for the two dry days. One of my disciples came to me and reminded me of what a great thing it was that God strictly heard our prayers. I told him we are sons of God.

In another instance, I was walking in the villages around my house witnessing to the villagers about Christ and calling them into the kingdom of God. I walked into this particular home which had dogs. Now in my life if you talk of dogs in another's home, I will stay away, particularly when the dogs are loose and their owner isn't by. No sooner had I stepped beyond the gate than the dogs, about four of them, huge scary German Shepherd dogs came up from behind the house in the compound and growled and barked charging at me.

My first instinct was to run. I almost fainted. Then, a sudden authority came all over me and I felt my hair stand on their ends. I raised my hand at the beasts who were now a meter away from me and shouted, 'Stop!'. As if hit by something, the dogs just braked instantly, looked at each other and backed off wagging their tails in a friendly fashion. I walked into the home, found an old man and preached Christ to him. He believed and got saved and I went on. It has not always been like this but these sporadic occurrences of dominion over creation must be common practice in the day to day lifestyle of sons of God.

Sons of God must rise and speak to the storms, deserts, famines, droughts, HIV/ AIDS, cancer, leukemia and tell them, 'Stop!' Sons of God must rise at the word of the Father and speak to corruption and rottenness in society, and speak to tribalism and nepotism gnawing mercilessly at our social and national fabric, and tell them, "Stop! Peace! Be still!" God is raising sons in the earth so that once again His sons can have dominion over all His creation; to restore and rule them.

- *Sons are the connection between heaven and earth.*

Like I had earlier said, the Father resides in the sons, and we know God lives in heaven. Yet these sons are placed on the earth. So, in the sons, both the realms of heaven and earth are reconciled into one. When Jesus taught them to pray, He did it on the basis that they were sons to the Father. He told them to say;

"Our Father who art in heaven."

Our Father; not our Master, or, our Lord. A Father has sons, a master has servants and a teacher has disciples. Prayer is a communication of relationship; of father-son relationship.

Sons ask, servants wish

"You are My Son; ask of Me and I will give you . . ."

The Father is committing to the son. He is telling Him to ask. This is because only sons have the right to ask anything of the Father. So Jesus teaches sons to ask the Father who is in heaven for the kingdom. Because,

> ". . . it is your Father's good pleasure to give
> you the kingdom"
>
> Luke 12:32.

When sons ask for the kingdom to come to earth, it happens. They are the ones with the keys, the ones who bring heaven to earth and destroy the curse that separated them after the fall.

When a son prays, he is asking. And when he asks, he receives because he delights himself in the Father and His will. However, when a servant prays, he wishes and because it's a wish, it can be granted or denied. So this decides

71

how each of them will come. The son comes confidently, knowing it is the Father's good pleasure to supply all his needs with a pat on the back. As such, a son comes with worship and adoration and thanksgiving when he comes to ask for anything from the Father. He knows he shall receive the very thing, not something like it.

When a servant comes, he comes fearfully and hesitantly, full of tears and pleas and hoarse shaky voice, knowing that he can be granted with a warning, or denied with a beating on his bare back.

A son knows the will of the Father: he is in the bosom of the Father; he knows His heartbeat, His pleasure. He comes with assurance in faith.

> "And this is the confidence we have in coming to God, that if we ask anything according to His will, He hears us. And if we know He hears us, whatever we ask, we know we have received of the Father."
>
> 1 John 5:14-15 nkjv

"Thy kingdom come, thy will be done on earth as it is in heaven."

Sons have the keys to the kingdom of heaven and so can open up heaven into the realm of men on earth. Again the authority that apostles were given by Christ is the authority of the Son; and sons are of and in the Son.

Sons of the Father bring down the rule of heaven, the spiritual realm of the Father, to impact and transform and remain on the earth. When heaven comes to earth, the throne comes to the house and a home is made.

> ". . . and we will come to him and make our
> home with him."
>
> John 14:23 nkjv

The heavenly beings start to appear to humans on earth because the difference between heaven and earth is removed and the two are brought into one in the Son. Angels, the spiritual beings that are assigned by the Father to keep us in all our ways begin to appear in meetings. I have read of many stories of men and women who saw angels or in whose meetings others saw angels.

I have been aware of angelic activity in my life very often and I thank God for this. Many times I would misplace something in the house and am in a hurry. All I would do is ask the angels of God to show me where I put it and, there, I shall go and get it. I have been woken up from sleep in the morning by a continuous knock on my bed until I thought people invaded my house, only to wake up and see nothing, nobody.

Some time ago, while doing an apostolic class in a village called Shiatsala, I was teaching on, 'The Magnificence of Redemption' and I had gone with a team from Kakamega. One of my team members came to the front at the end of the session and said that she saw a man standing by me all the while I was teaching, dressed in white flowing robes and looking very handsome. I could only conclude that it was an angel of God. As the sons of God rise in the earth, these occurrences shall be *usualities* and nothing shall be incredible about them.

This is the responsibility of sons; not of preachers. People who believe that for things to happen they have to really work hard and sweat it out, are serving with a servant mentality. By the end of the day, they always thumb their chests in self appreciation for a job well done. Even when their mouths seem to give glory to God, inwardly they are saying, 'were it not for me and my hard work, my prayers, my forty days fasting, my diligent study. Were it not for my powerful preaching, my gifts, my hands laid on her, it would not have happened'.

The whole church needs to come into sonship so that the mystery of God's will can be revealed and fulfilled. Eph 1:9-10.

When Jesus taught us to ask, He did this on the understanding that we are sons. Only sons are allowed to ask;

> "You are My Son, this day I have begotten You.
> Ask of Me and I shall give the nations as your inheritance . . ."
>
> Psalms 2:7-8 nkjv

> ". . . which of you, when your son asks for bread, you give him a stone . . ."
>
> Matt 7:9-11 nkjv

> Elijah said to Elisha, "Ask what I shall do for thee . . ."
>
> 2 Kings 2:9

> "And whatsoever ye shall ask in My name, that I will do, that the Father may be glorified in the Son."
>
> John 14:13

> "And I will ask the Father and He will give you another Comforter . . ."
>
> John 14:16(NKJV)

When a son asks, he receives what he asked for, because a son lives for the father, not for himself.

When a servant asks, he may be denied or given in limited measure, because a servant asks to use in exchange for his services;

"I have served you all these years and you never gave me even a goat to celebrate with my friends." This was the voice of a backslidden son; a son with a servant mentality.

- *Sons come to and bear the glory of the Father*

Jesus the Son came into this world full of glory; the glory as of the only begotten of the Father, full of grace and truth.
When God created the first two sons, they were 'crowned with glory and honour.' Sons come in the glory of the Father.

Jesus is the Father bringing many sons to glory.
When God swears;

> "But as truly as I live, all the earth shall be filled with the glory of the LORD."
>
> Num 14:21

The basic truth and reality here is that God shall cover the earth with His sons.
Glory is of the Father and is given to His sons. Jesus gave to the church the glory that the Father gave Him. This glory is in us but shall only be revealed in us as we walk as mature sons of God. With Christ in us, we hope for the revelation of this glory as we grow to the measure of Christ's full stature. The revelation of the glory in the sons is called the manifestation of sons.

> "And the glory which thou gavest me I have given them; that they may be one, even as we are one:"
>
> John 17:22

> "For I reckon that the sufferings of this present time are not worthy to be compared with the glory which shall be revealed in us."
>
> Rom 8:18

Jesus intends to present "to Himself a glorious church . . ." This glorious church is being raised from the inglorious one which exists today, which is in bondage in 'Egypt'. It is going to be a manifest company of sons who are now revealing, showing, expressing the glory in them from the Son.

- *Sons bring redemption to all creation in bondage since the fall*

> "For the earnest expectation of the creature waiteth for the manifestation of the sons of God . . . . Because the creature itself also shall be delivered from the bondage of corruption into the glorious liberty of the children of God."
>
> Rom 8:19-21

When God's sons fell into sin in the garden of Eden, creation fell with them. This was to be expected because when the Father created all the creatures, He placed them under the dominion and care of His sons. It's His sons who named all creation, thereby deciding their identity and determining their destiny.

When the sons fell, creation fell with them. When they lost dominion, creation rebelled to the sons who had lost sonship and had now become slaves, servants in the bare earth. Animals became wild and sought to harm their former king. The earth withheld its fruit and yielded thorns and thistles and the surface of the earth hardened as it developed thick skin. It now took great effort to till it in a bid to plead with it for its yield, but it gave too little. The curse was in motion and has been there until now.

> "For we know that the whole creation groaneth and travaileth in pain together until now."
>
> Rom 8:22

The rise of sons of God in the earth is hope to all creation that they too shall rise again from the curse of futility that the Father subjected them into; for He did so in hope. The hope that one day, yes one day, His sons shall return home and once again be crowned with glory and honour and shall manifest His glory to all creation and all creation shall rise from the suffering and pain they are in.

This is what makes the Father 'desperate' for sons in the earth.

Creation awaits the rising of sons. As a result of the fall, man lost the glory and so the world was plunged into darkness. Not only that but man also lost the blessing of the earth and had thorns witnessing against him, against his disobedience. The earth lost its fertility and the world lost its light.

In the restoration of sons, the words of Jesus get fulfilled that He spoke to the believers:

> "Ye are the salt of the earth . . . . Ye are the
> light of the world . . . ."
>
> Matt 5:13-14.

Sons heal the land and illuminate the world under the wicked sway of diabolical darkness. Wickedness and barrenness of the earth reign because mature sons have not been manifested in the earth. But all is not lost, there is hope and God subjected creation into the bondage of futility in hope. Sons of God are emerging in the earth and already we have begun to see isolated instances of restoration of creation through the glorious manifestation of sons of God in the places where they are. These instances are going to grow and increase until they cover the whole earth.

The new earth is already emerging in the earth. As sons get back to the throne of dominion, their word shall call back the fallen, rebellious creation to life and order, and it shall obey. The name and destiny of all creation is in the hands of sons of God in the earth. We should keep our eyes open and walk in obedience so that our obedience can be perfected to enable us punish all disobedience. This is the time and season for sons of God to arise and shine in the earth.

- *Sons have inheritance in the Father*

This cannot be overstated. Sons are heirs of God and joint heirs with Christ.

Our inheritance is in Christ, the perfect and pattern Son. Christ inherits as son of Abraham and as son of David. As Son of David, he inherits the throne of God and rules over the Father's kingdom. As Son of Abraham he inherits the land; the nations and all that is in them. This blessing of Abraham comes upon us through Christ. We must be fully baptized into Christ to put on Christ as a key to this blessing.

> "Christ has redeemed us from the curse . . . . that the blessing of Abraham might come on the Gentiles through Christ Jesus; that we might receive the promise of the Spirit through faith."
>
> Gal 3:13-14

> "Now to Abraham and his Seed were the promises made . . . , And to thy Seed, which is Christ."
>
> Gal 3:16

Christ is the Seed or Son of Abraham to whom God made the promises of inheriting the land. This makes Christ heir of all things that Abraham was promised.

> "And if ye be Christ's, then are ye Abraham's seed, and heirs according to the promise."
>
> Gal 3:29

> "Therefore, thou art no more a servant but a son; and if a son, then an heir of God through Christ."
>
> Gal 4:7

In Christ the Son, we are Abraham's seed just as Christ is Abraham's seed. In Christ, we inherit just as Christ inherits. This is the meaning of being heirs of God and co-heirs with Christ; that if we suffer with him, we might also be glorified with Him.

The Father's fullness is the sons' and all that is the sons' is the Father's. The inheritance from the Father is not something personal that you can pack in your backpack and leave with. Inheritance is shared without splitting it. It is the Father's and it is the sons'; not that it used to be the Father's but now it is the sons'.

When a son leaves the father, he has left home. He shall be in want no matter what he tries. He may get wages for working hard, or get gifts for looking pitiable, but not inheritance.

Inheritance is in the hands of the Father. It is not in the hands of the spiritual father either, but in the hands of the heavenly Father. Your spiritual father may try to bless you but your blessing comes from the heavenly Father. In fact the role of a spiritual father is to reveal to you the heart and fullness of the heavenly Father; bring you into a deep and lovely relationship with Him and leave you in His fellowship being led by His Spirit.

So Paul says to his sons in Corinth, "Follow me as I follow Christ". He further tells them that he looks "poor yet making many rich."

When the prodigal son asked for his goods that fell for him from the father he later decided to leave home and go to a far country. He sought for 'a home away from home'. In the father-son relationship, there can never be a substitute to home. This idea of alternative lifestyle does not come from God.

When he left home, he went with the flesh of his inheritance but the spirit of his inheritance remained with the father at home. The spirit is the source of the flesh and supplies to the flesh. He soon ran out of stuff, resorted to job hunting and at least got something, as a servant.

You cannot be a son away from home. You have got to be home to be a son. You have got to be, to be. You do not have to do, to be. So why is it that when the son strayed, the father stayed? Home loses definition in the absence of the father. Home is where the father dwells.

When a son leaves home and starts behaving like a servant seeking identity out there, the first reaction of the father is to stay home and wait. Wait in hope that one day, his wayward son will come home. And sure, like the prodigal son did, he eventually comes back home and receives a decent welcome; the past put behind them.

If this son takes too long to return home, based on the father's impatience, he might decide to do the second thing; send his son who is with him home to seek and find his lost son and bring him home. In this case, the father foots all the costs incurred; the cost of the transport, the cost of convincing the lost son, everything is on the father's bill. Still, the Father stays home.

This is what God did when He sent His only begotten Son. Jesus came with the full price for finding, buying back from slavery and transporting us back home. And by extension, this is what Christ our Father is doing by sending apostles to the church and nations; to find and redeem through the revelation of Christ the Son of God and restore His lost sons. This makes the apostolic ministry a sons' ministry.

Apostles, therefore, have to be fathers. One cannot be a father if one is never a son. Better still, one cannot be a good father if one was not a good son. You cannot give what you have not received. Some apostles who are already functioning still need to be fathered until the heart of the Father God is fully formed in them.

Peter Akeck

I was raised by some good people who were not the best fathers. As such, I grew up limping and with much heartache. I grew up with fears and insecurities and with a desire to prove myself and appreciate myself. When I responded fully to God's call to be an apostle and a spiritual father, I chose to submit my life and ministry to a senior apostle to help in bringing me up as a good son so that I may be a good father to God's sons He is raising through my hands.

For sons to be raised, fathers must be present and must make a home where sons can be restored to. If spiritual fathers are not in place, or if the so called spiritual fathers are excellent masters and 'pharaohic', God will not place His sons under their care but He shall still have sons. Father God can choose to raise His sons in the wilderness, like John was raised. Father God shall furnish tables in the wilderness before His sons, for their nourishment and safety. He will make rivers to flow in the desert. He will still carry out the divine design unhindered and bring many sons to glory in the earth.

Home is not going to heaven. Home is being where the Father is; the Father's house where He and His sons dwell in oneness.
We shall later look at the specifics of inheritance in chapter six of the book under the title, The Inheritance Of Sons.

CHAPTER FOUR

The Processes Of Sons

God created a son, loved him and gave him everything He had. This son disappointed Him when he fell for the temporal offer from the enemy. By so doing, man fell from sonship; from the level of honour, glory, dignity and maturity he was created in; became a servant and resorted to childish ways of living; being tossed to and fro, and being carried about by every wind of doctrine brought to him from the craftiness of wicked men's deceitful plotting.

> "For all have sinned and fallen short of the glory of God."
>
> Rom 3:23

Man changed a lot, negatively, but this did not change God.

So this fall rewound everything back and the process of raising him from the fall to the level he fell from began in earnest.

The processed product crushed but the process and the Processor remained intact, indented.

Mature sonship indeed is a long journey and a very demanding process. It starts way back at the point of our conversion, when we first believed and received the Lord.

> "But as many as received him to them gave he power to become the sons of God, even to them that believe on his name."
>
> John 1:12

This is where the process begins with us. At the point where we believed on the Lord after we heard the gospel of truth, were water baptized and received the Spirit wherewith we were sealed unto God against that last day, we got properly born from above into the kingdom of heaven.

At this point, we were little children, new in the kingdom of God and learning to walk in the newness of life in this new kingdom. Our first level of growth was the level of discipleship. It was time to lay foundations in our lives, help us to discover the dead works we carried over into this holy ground so that we could 'remove our shoes' to put on His new shoes to walk with Him. This is the elementary level of discipleship.

In this level a lot of re-direction takes place through disciplined reading and studying of the Word, learning to hear God and walking in obedience to His voice. It is the level of continuing in the word of Christ taught to us. This is the process of cutting us off completely from the world, with the renewal of our minds so that we can be able to discern good from evil and walk in the good, perfect and acceptable will of God.

The goal of discipleship is to bring us to a level where we are well grounded and solidly founded on Christ; where we are well versed with His word, and are able to teach others what things we have been taught. The key words in discipleship are *knowledge* of the truth and *obedience* to the truth.

The process then brings us to level two where we are now taught how to discover the gifts and callings of God in our lives. We are shown where our rightful places of functioning are in the Body of Christ and how to receive the grace of God.

This is the level where we are taught how to serve God and are hence made ministers. In this level we learn how to be good stewards of the manifold grace of God by using our gifts to serve the Lord and the Body.

Ministry is two fold; ministry to the Lord and ministry to the people.

Ministry to the Lord is also two fold; ministry through prayer and intercession and ministry through worship and fellowship with the Lord.

Ministry to the people is also two fold; ministry of the word and ministry to the felt needs.

Ministry to the Lord comes before ministry to the people, because it is the outworking of our ministry to the Lord that we minister to the people. We minister to the Lord in brokenness and minister to the people in authority: authority that flows from broken vessels edify.

We minister to the Lord as priests and minister to the people as kings. If we have not been with the Lord, we do not have anything for the people. It is what we received from the Lord that we deliver to the Lord's people.

> "I delivered unto you what I first received from the Lord . . ."
>
> 1 Cor 11:23(NKJV)

To train men into ministry, Jesus took a team of rough men on team and went with them wherever He went. They not only heard Him teach how to do the work but saw the

85

demonstration of the same when He practiced what He taught. This is the biblical pattern of raising people into ministry. It works better than a class arrangement where people have to finish a curriculum and then they get sent to ministry.

Apostles, Prophets, Evangelists, Pastors and Teachers need to take teams with them as often as possible, so that the trained can grow faster as they observe the leader. This is the level of equipment; of helping them discover the deposits of gifts in them, of helping them develop them to maturity, of helping them to identify their rightful places of functioning, and of giving them opportunities to express what they have learned.

This is the process of making men out of boys. So, *diligence*, *performance* and *responsibility* are key words here.

Then there is the level of coming to know the Father and stepping into placement as sons. This is a higher and more mature level than the first two.
This is because sons are meant to be able to represent the Father and so immaturity can really be their undoing.

Sons of God are those who have been well discipled in the word of the Father, they have experienced the works of the Father in their lives, and now it is time for them to know the Father and relate well and fulfillingly with Him.

It is good to be a disciple - it is the beginning; we have just come out of Egypt.
It is better to be a servant - it is the means; we will be able to handle the wilderness.
It is best to be a son - it is the goal; we are now ready to inherit.

As disciples, we are learners and the key word is 'what'.
As servants, we are labourers and the key word is 'how'.
As sons, we are heirs and the key word is 'who'.

Disciples rejoice in their salvation and this forms their testimony.
Servants/ministers rejoice in their gifts and accomplishments and these form their testimony.
Sons rejoice in their relationship with the Father and this forms their testimony.
So by listening to someone testify before others, you can easily tell the level and process they are in.

Disciples are given rest through grace.
Servants find rest through their labours.
Sons enter rest through revelation of the Father and the security and maturity that come with that.

Disciples talk of mercy.
Servants talk of anointing and power.
Sons talk of grace, truth and love.
Notice, you have more to talk of as you grow up.

Disciples build character; it is the foundation of their progress and continuity.
Servants build ministries; it is the foundation of their accomplishment and power.
Sons build relationships; it is the foundation of their inheritance and dominion.

Disciples talk of *knowledge*; the concepts they have learned.
Servants talk of *ministries*; the works they have done.
Sons talk of *relationships*; the One they have known.

Disciples say, *"I have"*.
Servants say, *"I can"*.

Sons say, *"I am"*.

Disciples *seek*.
Servants *knock*.
Sons *ask*.

Disciples desire *knowledge*.
Servants desire *understanding*.
Sons desire *wisdom*.

Disciples *want* to be.
Servants do to be.
Sons *be* to be.

Disciples discuss where they have come from.
Servants discuss what they are doing.
Sons discuss who they are in the Father.

Disciples walk after God; followers.
Servants walk with God; co-workers.
Sons walk before God; leaders.

Disciples go to school to learn.
Servants report to duty to serve.
Sons sit on the throne to reign.

Inheritance And Dominion

There is a great and significant correlation between inheritance and dominion. This is because you can only have dominion over what is yours and is under your care. So, in the book of Genesis, we see God creating all things in three key realms; in the sea, in the air/sky and on earth. Then He creates man and tells him to have dominion over all those realms and their fullness. Therefore, one must be placed as a son, become a mature son, receive inheritance and then walk in dominion over one's inheritance. As such, without the saints and church stepping into sonship, the same cannot walk in dominion.

Most of what has been taught to the church in modern history and today has put emphasis on raising the most anointed, the most powerful servants of God, doing great works of God. As a result, the blessing of sonship and dominion has eluded the church most of her time. The church has largely been powerful but, sadly, less authoritative.

Power solves things but authority edifies. Servants have power but sons have authority. Power causes things to happen, breaks through iron gates and forcefully bends resistance. However, authority watches over people and their involvements, decides their destinies and wisely guides them into their fulfillment. The latter is the explanation of dominion.

The effect of the church in healing the sick, casting out devils, preaching the word, offering effectual fervent prayer and intercession, has been felt worldwide in what is called revivals. However, the effect of the church in deciding destinies of nations and communities, in molding moral and godly leaderships of nations, monarchies, kingdoms, states, and fathering them in the purposes of God, is negligible. This is because a great percentage of church and her leadership has not come into appreciable sonship before the Father, who is "governor over the nations", to be given dominion over nations. We cannot rule over, literally, "shepherd", what we have not received as our inheritance.

> "Ask of me and I shall give thee the heathen
> (nations) for thine inheritance, and the
> uttermost parts of the earth for thy possession".
>
> Ps 2:8

Sons ask for nations. Sons are given nations as their inheritance. Sons have dominion over the nations they are given. Having dominion over the nations is expressed in making disciples of and fathering the nations.

As we go to the nations, are we going as servants of God whose power is needed to solve a need, or, are we going as sons whose wisdom shepherd the leaders and their territories? Indeed, many times, the nations shall be opened by the power we bear as servants of God and finally be given to us at the time appointed by the Father as our inheritance. Then we shall have dominion over them and father them.

David is a clear example. He first went into the palace because of his strong gifting on the harp. I mean, the boy played the harp in such a way that evil spirits left the demonized king! His power as a capable servant opened the door to the throne and ushered him before the great king. However, that strong anointing never gave him the throne.

Saul used David's strong gift and anointing to make himself feel better but never consulted him or his God in his administration or leadership. Up to this point, David was more of a servant than a son. With time, the "Governor of the nations" saw his loyalty, faithfulness, maturity, wisdom and character, and gave him the throne. Then he became a father to the nation. In fact he was such a father that even the Benjaminites, the descendants of Saul, were willing to come under his wings.

Joseph was a father to Pharaoh and by extension, to all of Egypt. He was a real son walking in his inheritance and having dominion over his inheritance. His two sons Ephraim and Manasseh went ahead and inherited Canaan but for Joseph, he had dominion in Egypt and enjoyed the real life there.

Elisha is another good example of a son with inheritance and dominion. From the time he caught the revelation of the father when Elijah was being taken away, he stepped into his placement as a son and went ahead to become a father in Israel. As a son he was given the nations and had dominion over them. He was a father to the king of Israel.

> "And the king of Israel said unto Elisha, when he saw them, My father, shall I smite them? Shall I smite them?"
>
> 2 Kings 6:21

Now in this time, God is restoring the revelation of the Father to the church through the apostles whom He sends. Once again, the church is being adjusted from just being barracks of well trained military cadres of God, to being a family of sons of Father God. This restoration is elevating the church practically to the level of walking in her inheritance; in the dominion of Christ here in the earth, over all the works of His hands.

> "Thou madest him to have dominion over the works of thy hands: thou hast put all things under his feet:"
>
> Ps 8:6

Sons In Discipleship

However, even as sons, we must never stop being disciples of Christ. We must increase and "grow in grace and in the knowledge of our Lord and Savior Jesus Christ" (2 Pet 3:18). We must always follow Him as excellent disciples, committed to His word daily and obeying His word revealed to us. Sons are led by the Spirit of the Father and it takes the word of God to have illuminated feet and paths. Jesus as a Son of God gave Himself to prayer and obeying the Father, memorizing the law and the Prophets.

He said to the Jews who believed in Him,

> "If you abide in My word, you are My disciples indeed."
>
> John 8:31nkjv

Apostle Paul writes to his son Timothy and tells him,

> "Till I come, give attention to reading, to exhortation, to doctrine".
>
> 1 Tim 4:13 nkjv

This kind of approach and lifestyle keeps our foundations checked and strengthened all the time and enables us to stand firm, immovable and established in the Father ; always bearing fruits acceptable to Him and offering aromatic sacrifices before Him. An essential foundational teaching that is continuous is repentance from dead works and faith towards God.

This is because as we grow up, we keep noticing things that are not consistent with the new level of our walk and relationship with God, and we have to turn away from them; having our conscience cleansed from dead works so we can serve the living God with a pure conscience. The closer our walk with the Father gets, the deeper our repentance becomes and the stronger our faith in Him grows.

In sonship our discipleship continues and thrives.

Sons In Service

Also, as sons, we must be awake to the reality of work; that sonship is not a license to lousiness and indolence, just because we have now ceased from our own labours and have entered the rest of the Father. Jesus, speaking as a Son says,

> "My Father has been working until now, and
> I have been working."
>
> John 5:17 nkjv

As sons, we willingly and joyfully offer ourselves as bond servants of the Lord: diligently given to doing what we see Him do and what He commands us to do. We must not slacken when it comes to doing the work of the ministry, using the grace and gifts deposited in and given to us freely; serving the Lord even as we serve one another, without being weary of doing good. For "we are His workmanship, created in Christ Jesus unto good works, which God hath before ordained that we should walk in them" (Eph 2:10). Like the farmer who enjoys working in his farm alongside his laborers, sons delight in serving in the vineyard of their Father, even though they know they own all things.

The inclination of the mind is most important here. Sons do not serve with a servant mentality but with a mental disposition of ownership. Sons do not learn as babies but as mature ones who always seek the excellency of the knowledge of their Father's will, so that they may perfectly walk before Him.

So my discipleship and my service are hidden in my sonship to the Father. I am a son who diligently learns from the Father and delights in doing His will and to finish that which He gave me to do.

SONS, LET'S PUT AWAY EVERY CHILDISH THING!

> "When I was a child, I spake as a child, I understood as a child, I thought as a child: but when I became a man, I put away childish things."
>
> 1 Cor 13:11

> "But as soon as this son of yours came, who has devoured your livelihood with harlots, you killed the fatted calf for him".
>
> Luke 15:30 nkjv

It is time to mature up as sons. It is time to show a distinction between sons and servants; be more secure and more composed and not hasty and self centered.

Sons Verses Sons

Both sons in the passage of Luke 15 had opportunities to talk to the father. The younger used his to concentrate on his relationship with his father and not to drag his elder into it in any way. He came in all humility and in true brokenness to mend fences with the father and improve relationships. He knew he had done wrong but he also knew that above that offence, his father had a heart of grace and love, and that he would listen to him. This is the heart of a true son.

The older used his opportunity to peruse through his own credentials and qualifications and to judicially compare with his brother's, which he shamelessly and heartlessly dragged into the dust. He vehemently and viciously assaulted his younger brother. He really distanced himself from any connection with his younger brother, to whom he should be a father-figure in the demise of their father.

Here is a lesson for sons to learn and be wise. Sometimes, while we may be busy accusing and damaging our brothers before the Father, they may have had an earlier opportunity of mending fences with Him. While we are busy attacking their unpolished character, they are already accepted in the Beloved Son and are at the table enjoying the best of ribs. The elder brother thought he pulled a first one on his junior. He was late. The younger was already at home, being celebrated and celebrating the goodness of the father. Sons must spend most of their time with the Father building their relationships with Him, instead of accusing their brothers to the heavenly Father. As sons, we must put away childish things and grow up and become fathers. Fatherhood is not in the title, it is in the heart expression and the relationship we build unconditionally. There is nothing and no one to own. We are called to a life, into a family where we all happily belong and are secure. While we are still busy accusing one another to the father, trying to outshine one another, laboring to prove our worth in terms of our decorated service and accomplished performance, seeking the best seats and preeminence among our brothers, and loading it on the rest, are we not still acting as mere servants or insecure in who we are?

Are we not conducting ourselves as we did while we were in the house of bondage; when all we knew was survival and staying afloat no matter the situations; when we could use every trick in the book to send under currents, supplant and "dry clean" our brothers and remain the star -all in the hope that we shall be the darling and favorite of the father? The elder brother of the prodigal son was busy accusing his younger brother to the father, may be so that the younger may be seen as an unsuitable son and be disinherited so that he, the elder, would assume fully the inheritance from the father.

As sons who seek to come to maturity, we must not accuse our brothers to the father and walk in insecurity. We must evaluate our hearts and ask ourselves, "If the father has received him just as he is, who am I to judge and discriminate against him?" We must seek and love and restore our brothers to the warm fellowship of home in the father's presence.

Sons Verses Fathers

"And Noah began to be a farmer, and he planted a vineyard. Then he drank of the wine and was drunk and he became uncovered in his tent. And Ham, the father of Canaan, saw the nakedness of his father, and told his two brothers outside. But Shem and Japheth took a garment, laid it on both their shoulders, and went backward and covered the nakedness of their father. Their faces were turned away, and they did not see their father's nakedness. So Noah awoke from his wine and knew what his younger son had done to him. Then he said:

'Cursed be Canaan; a servant of servants he shall be to his brethren'."

Gen 9:20-25nkjv

"A son honors his father, and a servant his master. If then I am the Father, where is My honor .. ?

Mal 1:6 nkjv

The relationship between sons and their human fathers; be they natural or spiritual, is one that must again be wisely addressed, for through it, the heart of the heavenly Father is revealed and received.

This Man Father Noah

Noah's nakedness was his "in-tent affair"; only those within his tent, and at this point in time, Noah and his wife, and may be by extension, his sons and their wives, were privy to this. So to begin this delicate topic, Noah was within his territorial boundaries when he became uncovered. As such it was not shameful within the tent. It is logical to think that it is only within one's own tent that one's undressing can be addressed and dressed. Let's take drunkenness out of this for a second: who gets ashamed when undressing in his own bedroom? However, it is shameful when your little boy goes out there and in all innocence and unchecked frankness, tells the older siblings of your "design".

Sons must be cautioned against being caught in the temptation of discussing their father's nakedness, like Ham did to his father Noah, and was cursed with his posterity upon the earth. Sometimes, our fathers do things which are, in our eyes, blatantly off and we feel let down and hastily begin to think like either confronting them or telling others about it to talk to them. From the Book of Genesis, we learn that God's response to sin is first of all positional. That is why He asked Adam where he was before He dealt with what he did. That is why Aaron did not get judged immediately but was judged later when he left the priestly office.

Let's get back to the case of Noah. What did Noah *do*? Noah was drunk, true. He was naked in his tent, checked. It was the truth, checked. Somebody needed to do something about it, absolutely. But, *who* was Noah? He was the young man's father. He was a righteous man in the eyes of God. He was a man of favor with God. He was the man whom God delighted in and chose to build an ark of salvation. He was the one who built the ark that saved the young man's life. He was the priest of God who built the first altar to God by revelation. He was the strong leader who gathered all the animals in the ark and saved posterity. He was the vision (seed) carrier whom God made the covenant of the generations to come with.

Seasons of Awakenings for Drunken Fathers

The young man Ham owed his father as much, and more, than what he served him in his time of weakness. Remember, Noah "awoke" from his wine, and "knew". He did not stay drank and uncovered forever. And he awoke with sharper gift of knowledge. This is more powerful than revival. It is exaltation. Noah woke up a notch higher than before he fell drunk.

I feel strongly in my spirit even as I write this right now, to dedicate this portion of this book to all fathers; biological, adopted, step or spiritual fathers, and more specifically to those of them who have been battered in life; confounded and confused. All the fathers who have been carried away into any kind of drunkenness and embarrassing excesses; be they ministerial, sexual, financial, marital, or otherwise. You have been through so much you feel you are lying down uncovered in your tent, like Noah. Some of your sons and those who looked up to you as a model, have felt very let down and heartbroken and have spoken things they would not have said about you to others. You feel like crushed, your heart is empty and bleeding and you do not know where to start.

To you a say this: God is first and foremost a Father before He becomes anything else. God knows you and how much you have been through, and He is not condemning you, even though some of your sons and friends have condemned you. You are not drank beyond His awakening or beyond His reawakening. There is hope for you in Father God!

There is hope for fathers from the Father. The Father in heaven shall awaken them from their fallings and failings and shall place them on a higher dimension of operation and authority. At that time, whomsoever they shall curse shall get cursed into bondage, and whomsoever they shall bless, shall get blessed into fulfillment.

Your father shall awake from his wine and what shall he say to you, O naïve son, in the seasons of his awakening? If Noah awoke from his wine, and Samson's hair grew again, and Lazarus walked out of the tomb, and Jesus rose from the dead, surely, as these witnesses live, your father's situation shall turn around. Who Noah was, secured him and put the young man's judgments out of jurisdiction.

Our fathers, though not perfect, have been used a lot by God to bless, pray and fast, visit and encourage, provide and supply, cover and protect, nourish and feed, direct and edify our lives. In their strong times, they have stood with us and helped us immensely and our mouths have thanked them. Now, when their weak times come, we must maintain our faithfulness, like Ruth did. When Naomi became a shell of her former self and was surrounded with poverty, bewilderment and graves, Ruth still honored her "father", her mother in-law.

Technically speaking, we owe our fathers our very identity; for by them we have come to know Him who is from the beginning, even the Everlasting Father. We must honor them. We sons must repent of all undue words we have spoken against our spiritual fathers. We must repent of all the "in-tent truth" we intentionally spoke out there; about their moral standings, families, ministries, handling of resources, or otherwise, for by going and telling others "outside", we covered them with shame. We deliberately "crossed the brook Kidron" and went beyond our designated estate.

> "And the angels who did not keep their proper domain, but left their own abode, He has reserved in everlasting chains under darkness for the judgment of the great day."
>
> Jude 6 nkjv

> "And the king sent and called for Shimei, and said to him, 'Build yourself a house in Jerusalem and dwell there, and do not go out from there anywhere. For it shall be on the day you go out and cross the brook Kidron, know for certain you shall surely die; your blood shall be on your own head'."
>
> 1 Kings 2:36-37 nkjv

Noah woke up from his drunkenness and knew what his younger son had done. What do you think would be your spiritual father's reaction when he wakes up—for he shall surely wake up and rise from that nakedness—and hears what you went out saying? Will his heart praise you or condemn you? Noah cursed Ham's seed, Canaan. He made them servants for their brethren forever. Ham fell from grace and dominion and became a servant. He lost inheritance, just like that. His seed became perpetual enemies of the Lord's sons and were disinherited and their land given to the sons of Israel. Solomon put Shimei to death the day he arose and crossed the brook Kidron. God chained the angels who left their domain and strayed yonder. Whatever, the reaction, these fathers did not have favorable words or palatable reactions against those who went beyond. It is not a blessing to speak of the nakedness of fathers. Do not jeer or sneer or boo or reprimand or gossip about a father in your life, in their times of weakness. Remember, they shall sooner than later come into seasons of awakenings and exaltations, and what shall become of you?

Covering The Fathers' Nakedness

The younger son "went out" and covered his father's nakedness with shame and sorrow. The two older brothers "went in" and covered their father's nakedness with their backs and blankets. We must decide soberly what covering we are going to use; whether it's going to "S and S" or whether it's going to be "B and B". After the occurrence of the nakedness of the fathers, whether we walk from the scene or to the scene, we are releasing a "covering" upon our fathers.

As sons, we need to cover our fathers' nakedness, like the two elder sons—Japheth and Shem—did. We cover them by our prayers of love for them. We cover them by looking away from their nakedness, that is, keeping our attention and concentration on what God is doing. We cover them by holding our horses and not being sucked into talks about their nakedness.

> "A son honoreth his father…"
>
> Mal 1:6

The diversities of the levels show their interdependence and not their expendability.

As we step into sonship at the appointed time and by the revelation of the Father through the spirit of Sonship, we step again into a level with processes.

Sonship is supposed to be a level of maturity and honour, because it is the level of fully revealing and representing the Father. This is not always the case.

This is because as sons, again we begin to grow from immaturity to maturity, to the level where we have fully come to the measure of the stature of the fullness of the pattern Son, Christ.

It is within the open roof, wall-less walls of father-son relationship that inheritance can be discussed.

In this level we shall look at how God's sons behave in three different levels, namely; the young son, the growing son and the mature son.

We shall use the text of the parable of the lost son in Luke 15:11-32, as our base for studying the first two sons and Jesus as the picture of the full son.

The Young Son.

-He demands inheritance, 'Give unto me the portion of goods that falls unto me."

-He is aware he is a son and so uses his right to get what he believes is his.

-He is not aware of the appointed time by the father and so acts haphazardly.

-He is ambitious and full of youth. Soon he finds home boring and seeks to explore the outside world.

-He still struggles to know the heart of the father.

-He is thirsty for freedom and is self centered.

-He does not still value close communication with the father.

-He is still not clear on his destiny and so goes to a far country, seeking a home away from home.

-Not responsible enough over property. He wastes his entire livelihood on reckless living and rioting.

-He is still not disciplined with his life and falls short of the father's stand of holiness.

-He engages in reckless sex and so defiles the house of the Father.

-Still struggling with identity; joins himself to foreigners to be helped by foreigners.

-He forgets to cry "Abba, Father," and seeks to return to a master who would make him a servant.

-Still wants to prove himself and so comes to the father with a testimony of deeds.

-Is repentant and willing to continue and grow up.

-His inheritance is limited by the father as his growth is watched closely.

The Growing Son

-Abides home, not jumpy and adventurous as the younger.

-Is excellent in service and seeks praise for his works, still struggling with servant mentality.

-Still consults servants more than the father, not yet built a good relationship with the father.

-Occasionally lacks confidence in himself and needs reassurance from the father.

-Very possessive and would not want what he worked for given to another.

-More work oriented.

-Very teachable and easily breaks.

-Still struggles with the reality and revelation that all that is the father's is his.

-Continues to develop responsibility over the father's house.

-Is fully aware of his inheritance but lacks the courage to utilize them for the father's good pleasure.

-When sent carries the responsibility very well.

-He has revelation of sonship but no realization.

-Is caught between an excellent servant and a good son.
-He serves his father well with honour.

The Mature Son.

-Christ is the picture of the pattern Son that we all aspire to be.

-He never goes anywhere; He is sent only.

-He has dominion over the birds of the air, the fish of the water, the cattle on the land and over every creeping thing that creeps upon the face of the earth.

-He is heir of all things.

-He is the voice of the father.

-He is the brightness of the father's glory

-He is the express image of the father's person.

-He is the executer of the will of the father.

-He does not speak his own words but those of him who sent him.

-He only does what he sees his Father do.

-He minds the father's business.

-He correctly reveals the father.

-He walks in the authority of the father.

-He is a father and raises many sons.

-The father is well pleased to be fully found in him.

-He builds the father's house.

-He knows the will of the father and does it with satisfaction.

-He points others to the father.

-He transforms his environment.

-He is not under the law but is led by the Spirit of the father.

-He does well and finishes the work he is given to do.

-He serves with a sense and mentality of ownership.

-He belongs to the family of the father and so is secure.
-He receives the rebuke of the father with pleasure for he seeks to please the father at all times.

-He desires to see many come into the fullness and glory of the father.

-He shares the father's abundance with his brethren.

-He knows who he is and is secure in that.

-He readily receives discipline and improves his quality of sonship.

-He has an acceptable standing before the father.

-He has unlimited and eternal inheritance.

God's goal is not just to have sons for the sake of it but to have a quality of sons that He is proud to be identified with and to whom He can publically say;

"These are My beloved sons; in whom I am well pleased."

He wants to fully be found manifested and represented in His mature sons all over the earth. It is time for those of us who have already come into sonship, to move on to perfection as mature sons according to the Father's threshold.

Let me summarize seven things from the qualities under the mature son:

i) He has the **spirit** of the father. This is the key to likeness of the father.

ii) He has **courage** from the father. This is the key to excellence in serving the father.

iii) He has **identity** in the father. This is the key to destiny with the father.

iv) He receives **discipline** of the father. This is the key to godly character.

v) He is **secure** in the father. This is the key to permanence.

vi) He has an **inheritance** in the father. This is the key to kingdom prosperity.

vii) He receives **dominion** of the father. This is the key to rulership.

It is time to press on into sonship: for those of us who have been operating only as servants or children of God. It is time to get the revelation of the Father and receive the Spirit of adoption by which we qualify for placement as sons before the Father. It is time to be sons unto the Father. It is time to come back home, and grow into mature trusted sons.

CHAPTER FIVE

The Sowing And Manifestation Of Sons

The Sowing Of Sons In The World

The processing of sons from immaturity to maturity brings them to the place whereby they are now ready for sowing into the world. This is now the apostolic dimension of going into all the world and making disciples of all nations.

Sons are not meant to be in the church setting; sitting every Sunday and being kept warm by the songs of the choir, then going home to their houses.

Sons are precious seeds made for sowing in the field called world. Sons are for the world, not for the church. The church setting is the environment for their growth and development into maturity. Once they attain this stature, the Sower descends on them, rubbing his hands together with a great grin on His face. It is sowing time.

Once they attain a good measure of maturity, it is time for them to be sent forth into the world. However, this also must be done after waiting on the Lord and establishing the timing and location.

Listen to the parable of the wheat and the tares;

> "He answered and said to them, He that soweth the good seed is the Son of man; the field is the world; the good seed are the children of the kingdom;."

> Matt13:37-38.

The Greek word for the word children as used in this verse is "huios" meaning "a son, a mature child".

Christ is sowing His mature sons into the world as seeds of His kingdom, to 'die and resurrect' in abundance of sons wherever they are sown.

"Unless a grain of wheat falleth to the ground and dieth, it abideth alone."

There are sufferings they shall endure; great temptations in the world and in the nations and persecutions from false brethren and anti-Christ systems and governments; but they must resurrect from all these in multiplicity of sons as enduring seeds.

The nations of the world are not waiting for evangelists to evangelize them. While evangelistic campaigns have born some good fruit in every city and in every country, and even broke open some very tightly locked nations, seasons have changed and we must be prophetic and apostolic in this season. Evangelization brought a great multitude into the fold.

God now is focusing His tools and energy on the raising and planting of sons into the world; sons who stand on their own and still be sons; sons who can go into a far country and not resort to prodigal living and foreign women; sons who will remain true to the Father and who won't compromise their testimony of the Lord, like Peter did when he went to the house of the Gentiles; sons who will walk into the cold waters of the world red hot, and walk out still red hot; sons who will walk into the dens and holes of wolves and come out victorious; sons who will make many like them from the world and not such who will become like the world.

The nations are waiting for this quality of sons of God to be planted in them. This is the Lord's doing and it is marvelous in our eyes. He shall choose where to plant His sons. When the armed soldiers of 'Amisom' pull out as the war against terror in Somalia comes to an end, the sons of God must prepare to pull in and occupy the land with the revelation of the Messiah and be firmly planted there.

Sons of God are called the trees of righteousness, the plantings of the Lord. Sons are wanted all over the world; Sudan, the Southern Sudan, Libya, Morocco, Niger, DR Congo, Rwanda, Kenya, Canada, Iceland, Green land, the Islands of the oceans and seas, The Islamic Republic of Pakistan, Australia, Iraq, Iran, Kuwait, Saudi Arabia, Kazakhstan, USA, UK, Sweden, Poland, Vatican city, Italy; the sons of God are need to be planted in these and indeed, in all the nations of the world.

As seeds, they will all have 'to die to reproduce'. This death does not necessarily talk of physical death but a real intense pressure upon their faith to the point they are overwhelmingly jaded and only God and faith in God keeps them going on to fulfill the great apostleship upon them in those nations. Some actually will die physically as martyrs.

This planting is not the going into the nations for a week; doing a meeting and then rushing back home to the warmth of your economy as you relax with a glass of wine in a Jacuzzi. That is for modernized missionaries. God is not raising these missionaries in this time.

He is raising sons who shall be planted and take root in the world where they are planted. Where the Lord shall plant you, there you shall make home. We must beware of the homesickness of the early church that kept them holed in Jerusalem no matter what, until God had to use intense persecution to scatter the church and plant it in the regions beyond what they knew as home.

So, dear sons of the Father, enjoy your nice built homes while you can, while you wait for the mention of your name as roll call is taken. You do not know where you shall be planted. Study the book of Acts and Apostle Paul shall be your teacher.

Jesus says that in every place the sons of the kingdom are planted, the enemy also plants his own sons. It is a battle for control of and dominion in territories, cities, villages, towns and indeed, nations. It is a battle for the heavenlies where those who occupy it rule the earth below and its happenings. So sons shall face off with sons; the good verses the bad. No matter the happenings in between, we know the end,

"Judgment was made in favor of the sons of the kingdom and to them was the kingdom and dominion given"

The whole church ministry must focus on what God is attending to. God's eyes are on sons going forth; not members being maintained. The church is not a maintenance centre but a making centre. The Father is pouring out and sending forth the Spirit of His Son into many hearts to transform them into sons of God; grown and mature, ready for planting in the world.

God wants to sow His kingdom in every world of this world. This kingdom is the potential life in the sons being sown. As new life sprouts out of a dying seed, so the kingdom of God shall be born in every place the sons are planted; the amount of persecution they face notwithstanding.

And that is just but the beginning.

The Manifestation Of Sons

God is looking for fruit, not just germination.

> "You did not choose Me but I chose you and
> appointed you that you might go and bear fruit
> and fruit that shall abide . . . ."
>
> John 15:16 nkjv

These sons He is choosing and appointing to the world must bear in their minds that their goal is to bear fruit.

The true test of the seed is in the quality of the fruit it produces from the ground wherein it is sown.

Let's put excuses of blaming the type of the ground aside. God is expecting fruit, wherever He plants us notwithstanding. He owns the seed and chooses the ground where to plant the seed. The good ground in the Parable of the Sower, had three different results. In one good ground it produced thirty fold, in another it produced sixty fold and in yet another, it produced a hundredfold. God did not blame the good soil that produced thirtyfold; neither did He say that was below expectation. Whether it was thirty fold or sixty fold or a hundred fold, the value of the fruit and the quality of the production are what He is looking at.

Your success is not in the abundance but in the quality of production you have. We cannot compete over these things. Pastors must enter the Father's rest and understand that to each one grace has been given according to the measure of Christ's gift. Like prophet Ezekiel found himself placed in the valley of dry bones and delivered, we must put excuses aside and deliver. The Father expects fruit from His seed sown in His field. The earth is the Lord's. The world is the Lord's field.

He expects fruit, but again, not any fruit. He is expecting fruit; that stands the test of time and weather, not that rots with time: that lasts the whole time, not that diminishes with time; that abides, not that is temporal; that remains, not that gets taken.

This quality of fruit is seen in the multiplication of the sons into multitudes of sons, and an increase and abundance of revelation of the kingdom in those places where they are producing. It is the radiance of the fragrance of the fruit, going forth and forward, reaching and changing wherever its fragrance reaches.

This quality of production reveals the glory of the seeds sown; their intricate potential which was manifold, now manifest on the face of the earth; taking, redeeming, freeing, transforming and restoring creation by its manifest fullness. This quality of fruit is what justifies and manifests the seed. It is called the manifestation of the sons of God. This is what all creation is waiting for.

CHAPTER SIX

The Inheritance Of Sons

Sons have inheritance from and in the father. The issue of inheritance of the sons is one which is deep and very involving, and the more I look at it the more I realize I have yet more to see. However, I will in this chapter share with you those aspects of inheritance that have been made clear to me.

- **The Father**

> "And if children (Greek word here is 'huios,' meaning 'son'), then heirs; heirs of God, and joint heirs with Christ ..."
>
> Rom 8:17

As heirs of God, we inherit God; we have Him as our inheritance. Christ came into this world as an heir of God. We are co-heirs with Christ of God.

A key aspect of the inheritance of sons is the Father. The Father is the inheritance of sons. The pursuit of a son's heart should be the Father; to know Him, to relate well with Him, to love Him and to be always found at home in Him. On this inheritance hang all the aspects.

Just like the Levites were not given any portion of the land because the Lord was their inheritance, the sons of God need to realize that they live for the Father and so the Father becomes their chief inheritance. Sons are partakers of the Father, their fullness is the Father. The Father is fully found inhabiting them. He is their inheritance.

Every son must committedly seek to pursue the heart of the Father so that he can always walk, work and war before Him, not after Him. Sons are heirs of the Father's name; they are known by the name of the Father. They bear the name of the Father and are called by His name.

> "If My people, who are called by My name (sons) shall humble themselves and pray and seek my face and turn from their wicked ways, then I will hear from heaven and forgive their sin and heal their land."
>
> 2 Chron 7:14

It is only the sons of God who can be used by the Father to revert the curse on the ground because that curse came upon the land as a result of sons' fall.

The Father is calling His fallen sons to return to Him in true repentance and relationship. Then He promises to forgive their backslidings. This forgiveness of their sins results in their restoration to the placement as sons again before the Father. Consequently, God says He shall heal their land. The restoration of sons marks the restoration of the land.

After Lot had parted from Abram, God showed Abram a dimensional land, which whether he looked upward or downward, or left or right, he would see. And God told Him that all the land he saw, he gave to him as inheritance. In essence God was saying, "All the land you saw when you looked northward is yours. All the land you saw when you looked downward is yours. All the land you saw when you looked to the left and to the right, is all yours". Abram saw something that filled all dimensions, something that stretched beyond the earth but covered all the spheres of sight. He saw fullness, a land without end. He saw a land in which the more he walked, the more he saw, and the more he saw, the more he was given. If he walked forever, he would see forever and possess forever. There were no limits, no bounds on the amount of land he would inherit. He saw something more than the physical land as we know it.

Apostle Paul, in writing to the church in Ephesus, also gives some dimensions of Christ. He writes about the church, Christ's body, being built up until she comes to the measure of the stature of the fullness of Christ (Eph 4:13). He writes of the breadth, and the length, and the depth and the height. He is writing of a fullness without limit and explains that when we come to this corporate comprehension, we "might be filled with all the fullness of God" (Eph 3:18-19). All the fullness of God dwells in Christ, for it pleased the Father that way (Col 1:19; 2:9). Christ is more than a person; He is a fullness. He is the sum total of all of God and all that we can ever see and walk in, in the Kingdom of God. He is our ultimate inheritance; the true definition of the land of our possession. In Him are hidden all the treasures of wisdom and knowledge. In Him we are complete, made whole and perfect and satisfied in every way.

- **The Kingdom of God**

Sons are called "sons of the kingdom". God gives His kingdom to those sons that He is well pleased with.
That is why sons are allowed to ask for the kingdom.

"Thy kingdom come; thy will be done on earth as it is in heaven"

The kingdom of God, the spiritual domain of God where He rules and reigns and occupies is given to the sons of God. The headquarters of this kingdom is the Church, rightly seated in Christ in heavenly places. Sons of God must first be able to understand this special domain and fully function in it. When sons inherit the kingdom, they reign with Christ in it. They are seated with Christ on the throne of God's kingdom. The kingdom of God comes to places where the sons of God are and have cast out the evil occupancy.

> "but if I (a Son) cast out devils by the Spirit of God, then the kingdom of God is come unto you."
>
> Matt 12:28

The kingdom of God is not eating and drinking but is righteousness (relationship of faith acceptable before the Father), peace (total restoration) and joy (fulfillment) in the Holy Ghost. We must as sons of the Father walk in these three qualities of the Kingdom of God to walk in our inheritance. Remember these three are realities and possibilities only in the Holy Spirit.

Sons must seek to daily and continually see the manifestation of the kingdom of God in their individual lives, in their homes, in their places of service or work and in their communities. The kingdom of God is their inheritance.

A son without inheritance is not a son. Because sons inherit the kingdom, they inherit dominion or authority. Dominion is authority 'over' and 'in' something or somebody; not 'under'. Dominion is God's plan to cover whatever submits to it and to influence whatever receives it. This dominion makes the son an executive king, not a figurehead. Sons are in charge and wield executive authority over the kingdom of God, beginning with church.

"But Christ as a Son over His (God's) house,
whose house you are . . ."

Heb 3:6

Sonship is not what we do; it is who we are before the Father. It is a position of relationship based and built on the revelation of the Father. This position of relationship is what gives sons authority because when sons are rightly aligned with the Father, the authority of the Father flows down into their hearts through the Father's Spirit and they rule and reign with the Father. This is where Adam was before they fell.

". . . . let them have dominion over . . ."

Gen 1:26, 28.

This was the inheritance of sons.

- **The Kingdoms of the Nations of this world**

In every nation under the sun today, there is a kingdom. There is a rulership going on in every society of men. This rulership, be it singular (a King) or plural (a President), needs to be overseen by the sons of God. I am not saying that sons should go into politics and run for the highest political offices in their nations. That is the least they can do, not the primary reason of their sonship.

Every leader consults an authority, receives advice from an authority and relies on an authority. That authority the leadership relies on and consults is what empowers and emboldens the leader. In fact it is what keeps and governs the governor. It leads the leader and shows the way to the one who shows the people the way.

The sons of God do not have to run for political office in order to change the nation. Even if they do, and that authority that leads the leaders is still in place, it will be the voice speaking in the life and work of the sons and they will soon find themselves acting like all the others before them.

Have we not seen good brothers in the Lord, even Christian ministers held in high esteem, running for high political offices with great promises to the electorate, only to get in there and be swallowed up in the status quo? Their former strong voices fighting for the rights of the people are now hushed into fat salaries and luxuries and nothing changes; it is business as usual.

Going into political office will not effectively change a nation if the sons of God do not assume their spiritual place of authority over the nations, in the heavens, and be the ones whose word rules the rulers of the land. It is not time for the demons to be the ruling principalities and powers over nations and cities and communities. It should be sons of God who are the ruling principality and power. The battle is for the heavens and it pits principality against principalities, power against powers.

> "In Him you are complete; who is the head
> of all principality and power."
>
> Col 2:10

That does not make Jesus the Chief Demon under which all the wicked powers and principalities operate. The principality and power mentioned here, and notice it is in singular, is the church; the mature son—church that has risen and grown to maturity and is executively seated with Him on the throne in the heavens, ruling the earth. God wants one authority over the land, and that authority is His authority; the sons of God in the heavenly places.

The truth is heaven rules the earth and the place of sons of the Father is in the heavenlies. The sons of God must be placed in the high heavens over the nations and their kings and presidents and Governors, so that no matter who becomes the king or the President or the Governor, it is the authority of the ones in the heavens, the sons of God, that shall influence and lead the leaders and decide their leaderships.

The garden of Eden was the garden of God and was a spiritually exalted place that was designed to rule all the earth. The sons of God are as a city built on a hill that cannot be hidden. Cities by geography were set on raised topography because cities served as regional watchtowers.

Philip went down to Samaria, displaced the ruling principalities and powers over Samaria and became the ruling principality and power. It did not matter who was the Mayor or Governor or Senator or witch or power in Samaria. Philip was in charge because he took possession of the heavens and got seated there as the one with dominion over Samaria. His word ruled Samaria. Everybody else including demons had to obey his word. This is how true mature sons of God need to be in every city and town and village and nation they are planted in. How did Philip succeed to do this? By preaching Christ (The anointed Messiah, the Son of God) to them, the manifold wisdom of God made manifest to spirits and flesh.

> "Then Philip went down to the city of Samaria and preached Christ unto them."
>
> Acts 8:5

> "And to make all men see what is the
> fellowship of the mystery . . . to the intent that
> now unto the principalities and powers in the
> heavenly places might be made known by the
> church the manifold wisdom of God."
>
> Eph 3:9-10

Look at Daniel, a spiritual leader in the heavens over Babylon. Whether it was Nebuchadnezzar or Belshazzar or Darius; kings came and kings went, but the word of Daniel ruled the kings and their kingdoms. This is the best example of the sons of God inheriting the kingdoms of the nations. A heathen king stood up and made a royal decree:

There is no other God to be worshipped but THE LORD"

As sons of God position themselves in their Father's kingdom and execute His authority at home well, the Father plants them into the whole world for the purposes of propagation; God wants His kingdom to take, change, make and rule all the kingdoms of the world. All systems of this world that govern people have been given to the sons of God to inherit.

Whatever field the Lord shall plant you, He expects you—using His kingdom presence—to take and make that field His territory. This is where subduing or subjugating comes in. Sons will have to exercise authority over rebellious kingdoms, displace the evil principalities and powers over them and become the ruling principality and power under the headship of Christ.

> "All the ends of the world shall remember
> and turn unto the Lord: and all the kindreds
> of the nations shall worship before thee. For

the kingdom is the LORD'S: and he is the
governor among the nations."

Psalms 22:27-28.

The realization of this culminates in the fulfillment of the
mystery of God;

'And the seventh angel sounded; and
there were great voices in heaven saying,
The kingdoms of this world are become the
kingdoms of our Lord, and of His Christ; and
he shall reign forever and ever."

Rev11:15

- **The whole earth**

The whole earth has been given to the sons of God
to inherit. The preaching of Christ is to be taken to the
ends of the earth. The gospel of Christ takes people and
their territories; the world (being lit) and the earth (being
salted).

The Father promises the Son;

"Ask of Me and I shall give you . . . . to the
ends of the earth as your possession."

Ps 2:8

"The heaven even the heavens, are the
LORD'S: but the earth hath he given to the
children of men."

Ps 115:16

Because the church has known servant-hood for a very
long time, the reality of inheritance has eluded it daily. As

servants, the church has been hopeful for a day it shall be relieved and taken out of this horrible earth to a place in heaven and they shall be comforted there while the devils rule the earth. Servants are always hungry for freedom, always anticipating a day when they shall be released to return home at the end of their slavery.

In these days with the revelation and restoration of sons, the truth is returning to God's people. This earth was created by God for God and His sons. Adam was created and placed on the earth. In this earth Adam experienced the fullness of heaven, for in him both heaven and earth met. Sons of God are being raised in the earth to inherit the earth. As co-heirs with Christ, we are given to the ends of the earth as our possession.

The righteous shall not be removed from the earth but the wicked; just as it was in the days of Noah.

> "They (the wicked) were eating and drinking, marrying and being given in marriage, and did not know until . . . . the flood came and took them (the wicked) all away. So shall it be in the coming of Son of Man. One shall be taken (the one who does not know) and the other (the one who knows, like Noah) left."
>
> Matt 24: 38-40.(brackets mine)

It is those who did not know, who were taken away into eternal destruction by the flood. Noah was not among them because he knew a flood was coming and in fact built an ark in high anticipation. Noah was NOT taken anywhere; he prevailed upon the storm and the flood on the earth. We must learn to allow the Scriptures to speak to us and not to speak to the Scriptures.

"And she conceived again and bore a daughter. And God said unto him, Call her name Lo-ruhamah: for I will no more have mercy upon the house of Israel; but I will utterly take them away."

Hos 1:6

"The righteous will never be removed, but the wicked will not inhabit the earth."

Prov 10:30 nkjv

"For the upright will dwell in the land, and the blameless will remain in it; but the wicked will be cut off from the earth, and the unfaithful will be uprooted from it."

Prov 2:21-22 nkjv

"Blessed are the meek: for they shall inherit the earth."

Matt 5:5

- **Glory**

Sons of the Father come into and inherit the glory of the Father. We came into this glory for the first time and had a taste of it at our conversion. This was the reversing of the effects of the fall in the garden of Eden, where man sinned and fell short of the glory of God with which he was crowned in the day that he was created. Sin and glory never balance; the appreciation of one is the depreciation of the other. When sin walks in the glory walks out. Sin brings in another idol to be worshipped and glory belongs to God.

As we increase in the revelation of the Christ, we behold His glory; the glory of the only begotten of the Father which is full of grace and truth. As we behold this glory, we are transfigured into His image; from glory to glory by the working of the Holy Spirit. The level of our transfiguration decides the quality of our likeness to Christ.

We must constantly grow in this glory from level to level until we all come; to the measure of the stature of the fullness of Christ; to the level we are filled with all the fullness of God; to the level we are presented perfect in Christ; to the level He can present unto Himself a glorious church.

Glory can simply be referred to as:

- The nature of God; His existence, His personality.

  John 1:18

- The fullness of God; His Opulence, his totality.

  Matt 16:27

- The worthiness of God; His excellence, His quality.

  2 Cor 3:18

- The revelation of God; His appearance, His identity.

  John1:14

- The representation of God; His countenance, His entity.

  1 Sam 4:21

- The accomplishment of God; His occurrence, His ability.

  John 2:11. Prov 20:29

- The rulership of God; His reverence, His authority.

  Ex 15:6

As we grow in the grace and increase in the knowledge of our Lord, the glory in us increases and multiplies. As we daily peel off the exposed layers of the old man, and get daily endued with the new man being formed in the image of Christ, we get more glorified.

> "Moreover whom he did predestinate, them he also called: and whom he called, them he also justified: and whom he justified, them he also glorified."

  Rom 8:30

We are heirs of His glory; of all He is and all He has; of all His fullness.

> ". . . that we might be filled with all the fullness of God."

  Eph 3:19

When we come to this point, we shall experience what prophet Ezekiel foresaw and prophesied,

> ". . . and the earth shone with His glory."

  Ezek 43:2

CHAPTER SEVEN

The Sons And The House

The Son of God came into this world to do many things, one of which was to build for the Father a dwelling place among men. In this Son who is the firstfruit from the dead, are many sons of God. We sons are found in the Son, for we are His fullness. So the following are true about sons;

- *Sons are the building blocks of the house of God*

- *Sons are the builders of the house of God*

- *Sons are the house of God*

- *Sons abide in the house of God*

- *Sons are over the house of God*

SHOWING THE HOUSE TO THE HOUSE

"So the spirit took me up and brought me into the inner court; and behold, the glory of the Lord filled the house . . . And I heard him speaking to me out of the house; and the man stood by me. And he said unto me, Son of man, the place of my throne and the place of the soles of my feet, where I will dwell in the midst of the children of Israel forever, and my holy name, shall the house of Israel no mere defile, neither they nor their kings, by their whoredom, nor by the carcasses of their kings in their high places. In their setting of their threshold by my thresholds, and their post by my posts, and the wall between me and them, they have even defiled my holy name by their abominations that they have committed: wherefore I have consumed them in mine anger. Now let them put away their whoredom, and the carcasses of their kings, far from me, and I will dwell in the midst of them forever. Thou son of man show the house to the house of Israel, that they may be ashamed of their iniquities: and let them measure the pattern."

Ezekiel 43:5-10.

"And if they are ashamed of all that they have done, make known to them the design of the temple and its arrangement, its exits and its entrances, its entire design and its ordinances, all its forms and all its laws. Write it down in their sight, so that they keep its whole design and all its ordinances, and perform them."

Ezekiel 43:11 nkjv

God tells the prophet to 'show the house to the house of Israel . . ."

God says when the house(the nation of God's people) gets to clearly see the house(the kind of house God wants to identify with) and repents, then 'show the house the entire design' of the house and its ordinances. The message is clear: a willingness to change based on the initial revelation of God's house opens up the people to get into deeper revelation of the house. The details of the entire design and its ordinances were only to be explained when the house gets ashamed and repents.

We shall not waste our time bringing forth deeper revelation to a house that is rigid and that believes all is well in its quarters. Deep calleth unto deep. The depth of people's hunger calls for deeper revelation.

Apostles and prophets in our time must clearly show the house (the design of the house that Christ came to build) to the house (the saints today).
The house of Israel which was supposed to be the house of God, had lost relevance and meaning. So God called on the prophet to describe, to reveal, to show;

"The design of the house and its arrangements, its exits and its entrances, its entire design and all its ordinances, all its forms and all its laws . . ."

The purpose was "so that they keep the whole design and all its ordinances, and perform them."

The main reason why God is calling on the prophet to do all this is because His house(people) had lost the understanding and the revelation of His house(dwelling place). The revelation of the house wasn't there. As a result everybody was trying to do something that could have been what God wanted to be done, for God.

It is clear that in the absence of revelation, direction is lost. God is Spirit, His directions are spiritual and they are spiritually discerned. So in the absence of revelation, men and women shall still be busy working; working for God, doing something in His name, that they wholly hope should be what He wants to be done. But in the absence of the show-light, the revelation, it might talk like it, it might look like it, it might be taken for it, but it is not it.

"They set their threshold by My thresholds, and their doorpost by My doorposts; and there was a wall between me and them . . ."

Men did something parallel to what God wanted but no matter how much they tried, two things are dangerously conspicuous here. One, God distances Himself from it and calls it your threshold, your doorposts. It was built for God with all zeal but God rejects it and doesn't inhabit it. God will not accept anything short of what He meant. That is why the true house must be shown to the house today. Two, God puts a wall between it and His true house. There is a distinction between our house that we build for God and His house that the Son came to build for Him. Things from our doorposts cannot cross over and smear the holy vessels in His house. Likewise, the riches and abundance of His house cannot flow to those in the fake house. A wall stood between the two to put away any chances of confusing one for the other.

This also brings our attention to the state of Jerusalem at the time of the Lord in the earth physically.

> "O Jerusalem, Jerusalem, thou that killest the prophets, and stonest them which are sent unto thee, how often would I have gathered thy children together, even as a hen gathereth her chickens under her wings, and ye would not! Behold your house is left unto you desolate. For I say unto you, Ye shall not see me henceforth, till ye shall say, Blessed is he that cometh in the name of the Lord."
>
> Matt 23:37-39

Like we had said before, Jesus came to this house to gather it through the prophets and the apostles He sent to it, but this house rejected them because it had its way of doing things. It ceased to be the house of God and Jesus called it, "your house, left to you . . . desolate"

Jesus says He wanted to use these two ministries to gather the children of Jerusalem under His wings the way a hen gathers her chicks under her wings but Jerusalem refused. The point here is the apostles and prophets are used as the wings of Christ to gather His church unto His bosom. Apostles and prophets do not own the church but gather the church in every place they go and are received to Christ; they build and heal the church into oneness. This releases the wing covering of Christ to His church; for safety. We know when a chick refuses to come under the covering of mom hen's wings, that chick will become lunch to the preying kites and eagles. These birds of the air—according to the parable of the Sower, are demons—shall prey on and devour all the church denominations and ministries that have resisted apostles and prophets.

No wonder then that such denominations and ministries teach and practice different gospel from God's word; having erred from the faith that was once and for all delivered to the saints and have departed from the simplicity which is in Christ. Such denominations are caught up in vain arguments and philosophies, explaining away the truth and power of God in Christ through the apostles and prophets. Their reward is clear and their end is decided.

"Behold, your house is left unto you desolate"

Jesus makes a very strong remark here. It is dangerous to reject the apostles and prophets whom He sends. When Jesus departs from His house because we won't allow Him to run it through His apostles and prophets, it becomes our house. It is no wonder when pastors talk of "my church", 'my pulpit", "my people", "my congregation." Any ministry or church that rejects Christ's apostles and prophets, belongs to men. In the absence of Christ, it still has the state-of-the-art technology system, ultra modern building, great choir and worship team, cozy seats, thick blue carpet, well tailored uniforms for the choir and ushers, beautiful sermons, air-con, the big congregations, etc: all things that make it to be praised and admired in the eyes of men. BUT in Jesus' eyes, it is desolate! It is empty! It is void! It is left! It is abandoned. It is forsaken.

It is un-inhabited and a place for jackals and foxes—not for saints of the Most of God.

> "In that day seven women shall take hold of
> one man and say, 'We will eat our own food
> and wear our own apparel; only let us be called
> by your name, to take away our reproach.'"
> Isaiah 4:1(NKJV)

This ichabod (inglorious) situation takes over the church, which now allows men to govern themselves, pursue their goals and interests and do their will; all in the name of God to make it look like church. Honestly speaking, most of what we call church isn't church at all.

This is because the fullness of the church is Christ and His revelation in the midst of His people. This is because there is no church, no house of God, if Christ is not at home. This is because the church is an issue of Christ and without Him the church isn't. The definition, in fact, the pronunciation of the word 'church' came from the revelation of who Jesus is.

So, prophet Ezekiel has his work clearly cut out. He must maintain a prophetic focus and direction and at the same time have an apostolic doctrine and practice. He has to be a prophet with apostolic properties to fully describe, and reveal, and make known and explain the true house to the house of Israel.

It is great to begin with simple things. The church is the house of the Father; the very pillar and foundation of truth. Anyone looking for and thirsty for truth, should run to the church.

> "But if I tarry long, that thou mayest know how thou oughtest to behave thyself in the house of God, which is the church of the living God, the pillar and ground of the truth."
>
> 1 Tim 3:15

> "But Christ as a Son over His own house; whose house we are . . ."
>
> Heb 3:6

We are the ones being built in the earth to become the house of God. Anyone who builds a house has a vision for that house. Either he wants to use it for business. But we know that was far from the intent of Jesus for building His church because we see Him chasing out of His house merchants and business men who had converted His house into a den of gamblers. Some people build a house to rent it out. This either, wasn't the reason why Christ is building a house, because we see Him cast out demons (illegal tenants) from his people. He makes it clear in the Scriptures that He himself doesn't have even a place to lay his head upon. Then there are those who build to dwell in, and this agrees with the vision Jesus has for His house. He is building His house in the earth so that He might have a dwelling place among men. What is passing today for the church is far cry of the true design and form and practice of the church, and must be shown the true church that Jesus came into this world to build; so that church can observe and become it.

God who is Spirit wants a dwelling place, a house, among men; to be housed in a body.

There have been two clear housings of God in the earth. The first one was and is Jesus. Jesus came into this world as a housing of God. All of God occupied and dwelt in Him and walked in the earth in His body.

For the purposes of God to be fulfilled in the earth, for God to walk the earth, He must be housed in a body. Jesus served this purpose very well, and as we have seen in the previous chapters of this book, sons house the Father and so Jesus as a Son came into the world as the housing of God. God is a Spirit and not a body, and for the Spirit to function in the earth and fulfill its desire, it has to be housed in a body. So God found a house in the body of Jesus, and God who is Spirit dwelt in a body of a man. This is incredible; that God who is omnipresent could be housed in and dwell in a man.

This is a great mystery of godliness. When Jesus walked the earth, He was God manifested in the flesh; God seen as a man. This is because the purpose of the house of God is to manifest it fullness, its content; the God in the house. So whoever met and saw God's house met and saw God. Those who touched this body touched God, for the body housed and manifested the God in the house of God. To Jacob He was called El-Bethel, the God of the house of God.

> "that is, that God was in Christ reconciling
> the world to Himself . . ."
>
> 2cor 5:19

When this body was leaving the visible dimension into the invisible, He prepared another body to visibly house God in the earth. I use the word 'another' here in the sense the word "another" is used in reference to the Spirit being "another Helper". It is "allos" in Greek and means, "one besides, another of the same kind, similar to". This new body, this "another body", is made up of mature saints, sons, and it's being built to house God because God is still looking for a house. As God was first seen in the earth housed in a body that fully revealed and represented Him; that all who saw that body, saw God in the flesh, so shall it be in these last days.

Yes, God shall again be seen in the flesh in the earth, housed in a body made up of sons. This body, like the first, shall be the exact revelation and representation of the invisible God. Whoever shall see this completed body walking the earth shall be seeing a revelation of God. This body is the manifestation of God in the flesh, on earth, among men and is called the church. The church is the manifestation of God in the earth. God is building a house, a church in the earth, that the world and all creation shall look at and gasp, 'Behold the LORD!' because it shall correctly reveal and manifest God in the earth.

The house of God is being built in the earth. As this process of building goes on, this great house is being built using small words; 'by', 'upon', 'in,' 'up to,' 'through,' 'with' and 'for'. These small words in the building process, all these seven small words are followed by the same word to complete the sentence, and that word is, "Christ."

The house is being built *by* Christ.

The house is being built *upon* Christ.

The house is being built *in* Christ.

The house is being built *up to* Christ

The house is being built *through* Christ

The house is being built *with* Christ

The house is being built *for* Christ.

Built By Christ.

> "He said to them, 'But who do you say that I am?' Simon Peter answered and said, 'You are the Christ, the Son of the living God.' Jesus answered and said unto him, 'Blessed are you, Simon Bar—Jonah, for flesh and blood has not revealed this to you, but My Father who is in heaven. And I also say to you that you are Peter, and on this rock I will build My church, and the gates of Hades shall not prevail against it.'"
>
> Matt 16:15-18 nkjv

It is good to begin by looking at the disciple Peter. He gets a revelation which connects what is standing in front of him with the Old Testament prophecies. He sees the fulfillment of the promise for a Messiah in the man they are following and boldly stands out to declare,

'You are the Christ, the Son of the living God"

This revelation changed Simon. Jesus' immediate response to what Simon saw and declared, was to change the fisherman.

"... And I say to you, you are Peter ..."

Those who are fit for using in the building process must be those who have been changed by the revelation of Christ; not just those who came into the Lord or know the revelation. This is how sons qualify where others do not. Not all stones transported to the building site get used in the building. Not all structures joined to the building in the process of the building abide there forever. Some of them are there as servants to serve the builders and the building and when the house is done, they are pulled out.

(Understand what Jesus meant in John 8:35). Not all gathered in the kingdom through salvation are suitable for building the house.

When saints gather together on a Sunday or any other day, that does not make that gathering a church? It is like when stones are gathered in a place, that gathering cannot be called a house. It is when the stones have been properly set in the design that a house emerges out of the stones. We have called a pile of stones a house and it is time to show the real house to the house of God.

The stones that arrived at the building site, the church centre, must undergo another change to qualify for building the house. This change is called growth; for Christ is building a house that will stand the test of ages.

"... I will build My Church ...."

Christ is the builder of the house. The Son is the builder of the house. We have to keep supplying the revelation and Christ keeps building His house.

This revelation is with all the fivefold ministers but it is to the apostle that the abundance of this revelation is given. When we receive and sit under an apostle of Christ, we shall be partaking in the abundance of the revelation of Christ and this shall cause a faster growth and building of the church. When revelation of Jesus as the Christ is rare, the building of the house gets slow and at times, stagnates. Jesus says, I will build My house".

We must allow Christ to build His house as he wants according to His design.

Built Upon Christ.

> "...Upon this Rock, I shall build My Church
> and the gates of Hades shall not prevail against
> it."
>
> Matt16:18 nkjv

Christ is building His church upon His revelation; the revelation of Jesus as the Christ. This reveals the king, the One anointed to be on the throne who was prophesied about by Nathan, by David, by Isaiah, by Ezekiel and by the angel who appeared to Mary the mother of Jesus, just to mention a few.
God promised David a son who shall build His house and this son of David shall also be called the Son of God and shall sit on the throne of His father David and rule forever.

The revelation of the King-Son is the foundation of the house of God. This is because the house of God is to be the place of His throne and the place of the soles of His feet. This revelation of the king pours out and becomes a kingdom wherever it goes; it spreads the king's rule and influence everywhere it goes. This kingdom spreads through the word of the King. The word of the King comes from the Church for the church is the house, abode and dwelling place of God. God takes the nations through His word spoken by the house.

> "Where the word of a king is, there is power:
> and who may say unto him, What doest thou?"
> Eccl 8:4

The church which is the house of God, as the pillar and ground of truth, becomes the sure foundation of the word of His power by which His kingdom comes and spreads in the whole earth. The church is not only the launching pad of the kingdom as it moves to the nations, it is also the revelation of the same and the means by which the kingdom goes forth into all the world. This church is not a gathering of believers, it is a house built of mature ones.

God rules the nations from His house. The King and His revelation is the foundation of the Church. And the church is the trigger of the kingdom to the nations and the King is the foundation of the house. It is the source of His word and His Spirit. The word of God goes forth from his house. The Spirit flows from the house. Ezekiel saw a river flowing from the temple whose depth and breadth increased as it flowed out. Revelation of Christ increases in the field as we obey and go out to be planted in the nations.

Let us consider the parable of the two builders:

"Matt 7:24-27"

The building that fell and the one that stood had three same tests and several things in common but only one thing apart.

They both had builders.

They were both built.

They were both finished.

They both had foundations.

They both had same kind of tests.

They both had same amount of tests.

The thing that was different was the kind of foundations that they stood upon. The one that fell stood on sandy foundation. The one that remained was founded on the rock.

> "For other foundation can no man lay than
> that is laid, which is Jesus Christ."
> 1Cor 3:10-11

This is a strong kingdom foundation upon which an immovable and unconquerable house is built.

It is the foundation that attracts the walls. The walls are where we find the saints after their proper equipping.
What attracts the people to you, minister of the gospel? When all the projects—to the widows, the orphans, street-children elderly—stop, and the PA system isn't there, and the nice building is not there and you do not have a car and other promises that you gave to the people do not materialize; will the saints still come to where you are?

I have always asked myself; why is it that we do not see big cars parked under a tree while their owners attend a service under the same tree? Why is it that Mercedes Benz, Chrysler, BMW, Rolls Royce, Jaguar, Hummer, CR-Vs, Prado and others in that class, only always park near magnificent buildings with state-of-the-art finishing and furnishings?

Does it mean that the rich of the society find it hard to identify with a "poor" church?

When Christ builds His house upon His revelation, whether material things are there or not, the people shall abide as long as the foundation Christ endures. The more people see Him, the more they shall be attracted to Him; irrespective of where He is. The wise men came from the east—these were not simple men but were such as were held in high esteem because of their credible work and academic accomplishments—to worship a baby who was born in a manger!

Let Christ attract the people to the foundation. Let's knock off this hullabaloo to gather the greatest congregation using every trick in the book. Let Christ the foundation be revealed and let the foundation attract those who love Him with a sincere heart.

We must allow Christ to be the foundation of the house. Christ is building His house upon Himself, revealed.

Built In Christ

> "Christ Himself being the chief cornerstone, in whom the whole building fitly framed together . . . ."
>
> Eph 2:20-21

Christ is the cornerstone in whom the whole building is fitted. The church is fitted in Christ. The cornerstone, technically, is the main stone of the corner of a building among the four or many corners, set upon the floor and all the walls are built in it. It is our horizontal relationship with Christ through each other; that as we reach out to and embrace others whom the Lord has yoked us with in His house, we are by extension reaching out to Christ and being fitted firmly in Him as His house. This is the power and essence of *koinonia*.

> "And they continued steadfastly in . . . .
> fellowship . . ."
>
> Acts 2:42

The intensity of this fellowship is that we see the Lord through the brethren. We share with the Lord as we share with the brethren. We love the Lord as we love the brethren. We give to the Lord as we give to the brethren. This is how we are built in the cornerstone. Without the Cornerstone, we cannot be built to become the temple and the habitation of the Lord in the Spirit.

> ". . . that ye also may have fellowship with us:
> and truly our fellowship is with the Father and
> with his Son Jesus Christ."
>
> 1 John 1:3

Apostle John says that when you come into fellowship with us, you have truly come into the fellowship with the Father and with His Son Jesus Christ. This is being built in the cornerstone and this is what keeps the walls together and abiding.

Built Up Into Christ

> "But speaking the truth in love, may grow up
> into Him in all things, which is the head, even
> Christ."
>
> Eph 4:15

The house is a dynamic and growing house, growing up to
a head and that Head is Christ. Jesus delegated leadership
but not headship. He remains the absolute head of the
Church. The head in heaven is connected to the body in
the earth. As the church rises in the earth through the
effective functioning primarily of the five ministry gifts
and secondarily by all the members of the body supplying,
it grows up into the Head. This places leadership at the
bottom, not at the top; it is the head which is at the top.
The ministers who serve and function in His body are
therefore placed strategically to speak the truth, the present
truth of the revelation of Christ that causes growth of the
body up to fully and maturely connect to the head.

Yes, the body is already connected to the Head or else the
body would be mutilated and dead. However, the fullness
of this connection is yet to be realized as the body grows
up into Him and fills all things that were previously filled
by wicked principalities and powers.

In the old wineskin of leadership, the church grows up into
the Bishop or pastor, or arch-bishop, or presbytery, who is
the head of the church. He is the final authority and his
word is taught in all his branches. He is more revered than
the Lord. This is men's doorpost set beside the Lord's
doorposts. When the saints look up, the Father wants them
to see Him without the eclipsing of human figures seated
in the places of God. The new wineskin leads from under;
lifting up every one to see, love, relate with and grow up

into and be fully connected to the head, who is Christ. The more the body grows up into Him, the more the body is fully made into His likeness and the more the body reveals Him.

Built Through Christ

> "that the world through him might be saved."
>
> John3:17

The purchase of the stones used in the building of the house is done through Christ. We will not even begin to build without the redemption of our souls and those of others who are to be the stones.

As we had said before, the fact that the stones arrived does not automatically qualify them for the building of God's house. There is need for them to undergo a further change of quality to qualify. This change is called growth. This growth is caused through His word.

> "Now ye are clean through the word which I
> have spoken to you."
>
> John 15:3

This continuous cleansing effect on the stones brings them to a level of qualification for building in the house.

As the house gets built, it needs to be protected from attacks and effects of the environment and satanic weather. Remember when Nehemiah was building the house of the Lord, he made the people build with one hand and carry weapons with the other. Furthermore, he set sentries at night to watch over the house. The building must be watched over and kept safe.

> "And now am no more in the world but these
> are in the world, and I come to thee. Holy
> Father, keep through thine own name those
> whom thou hast given to me, that they may be
> one, as we are."
>
> John 17:11

Through His word, the house is kept on course. Through His word, the house is kept together in the bond of peace. Through His word, the house is kept growing and nourished and supplied.

Should any defilement come upon His house, should any stone stumble on another, should any saint become weak in the wall, the word comes in to sanctify the affected to ensure wholeness and holiness unto the Lord.

> "I pray . . . that thou . . . shoudest keep them
> from the evil one . . . sanctify them through
> truth."
>
> John 17:15-17

When Apostle Paul saw this, he boldly concluded;

> "I can do all things through Christ which
> strengtheneth me."
>
> Phil 4:13

Because apart from Him, we can do nothing.

Built Up With Christ

We are living stones being built together into a holy temple. But we need to remember that without Him—the main Stone and Rock—we aren't. We are in this building together to become. So, let's put the structure in the right perspective;

> "Coming to Him as to a living stone, rejected indeed by men, but chosen by God and precious, you also as living stones, are being built up a spiritual house, a holy priesthood . . . ."
>
> 1Pet 2:4-5

The house is not being built down; it is not a grave. Only graves are built going down. The house is not being built into oblivion. The church is intended to overcome all obscurity, grow taller than the herbs of the field and become the choice and outstanding tree that all birds of the air prefer to nest upon.

We are being built up because we are a city that is set on a hill. We are a house that cannot be hidden. We are the pride of the nations. We are the mountain of God. Those who come to the church must arise and come up. Things and virtue flow down to all the earth from the church's exalted place of spiritual elevation.

God is proud of His house, the place of the soles of His feet and the place of His throne. He wants the world to see His house and be attracted to it. He is building it up.

Not only that but we are being built up with Christ. Both Christ and us are stones; Him, a living stone rejected by men; us, living stones, together we are built up to be the spiritual house of God.

We are together with Christ from the beginning of our life to the end.

We died and were buried and were raised up together from the grave with Him.

> "Even when we were dead in sins, hath quickened us together with Christ . . . and hath raised us up together . . . and made us sit together . . ."
>
> Eph 2:5-6.

> "Therefore we are buried with him by baptism into death . . . . Now if we be dead with Christ, we believe that we shall also live with Him."
>
> Rom 6:4, 8

> "And if children, then heirs; heirs of God and joint-heirs with Christ; if so be that we suffer with him, that we also be glorified together."
>
> Rom 8:17

> "I am crucified with Christ;."
>
> Gal 2:20

> "If ye then be risen with Christ, seek those things which are above, where Christ sitteth on the right hand of God . . . . For you are dead and your life is hidden with Christ in God"
>
> Col 3:1-3

All these verses above and many more in the Scriptures show clearly how our very lives are intricately woven in the very life and existence of Christ. Christ is a living stone and we are living stones. Together, we are being built up to become God's house.

Built For Christ

> "Husbands, love your wives, even as Christ also loved the church, and gave himself for it; that he might sanctify and cleanse it with the washing of water by the word, that he might present it to himself a glorious church, not having spot or wrinkle, or any such thing; but that it should be holy and without blemish."
>
> Eph 5:25-27

Christ is building His church for Himself: for His glory, for His eternal purposes on earth, for His will to be done through and for His eternal habitation.

He is building a church He shall be proud to finally present unto Himself: a glorious church. Jesus is not coming to glorify the church; He is coming to a glorious church, to present such to Himself. The house must be filled with His glory before He can present her to Himself.

The King of glory wants to present to Himself a house of His equal, a house of glory.

> "LORD, I have loved the habitation of Your house, and the place where Your glory dwells.'
>
> Psalms 26:8

> "All the flocks of Kedar shall be gathered to you, the rams of Nebaioth shall minister to you; they shall ascend with acceptance on my altar, and I will glorify the house of My glory."
>
> Isa 60:7

> "The glory of Lebanon shall come to
> you . . . . to beautify the place of My sanctuary;
> I will make the place of My feet glorious."
>
> Isa 60:13

Remember the house that is being shown to the house is "the place of My throne and the place of the soles of My feet." In Isaiah 66: 1, the prophet declares that heaven is God's throne and earth is His footstool, or the place for the soles of His feet. The house that Prophet Ezekiel is commanded to reveal, is one in which the throne and the footstool are brought together in it. God's house brings heaven and earth into oneness in Him, to fulfill the mystery of His will.

> "That in the dispensation of the fullness of
> the times, He might gather together in one
> all things in Christ(His fullness, the mature
> son-church) both which are in heaven and
> which are in earth—in Him."
>
> Eph 1:9-10 nkjv (brackets mine)

> "The voice of the LORD makes the deer
> give birth, and strips the forests bare; and in
> His temple (house) everyone says, 'Glory!'"
>
> Ps 29:9

The house that Christ is presenting to Himself is and must be a house of glory. No wonder then, that before He left the earth, He not only gave them the glory He had with the Father before the world began, but later He breathed upon them the Spirit of glory. How then do we get to become a glorious house worth Christly presentation?

This takes us back to the Old Testament so that we can observe some things about those houses God built and presented unto Himself. Whether it was the Ark of Noah, or the Tabernacle of Moses in the wilderness, or the Temple of Solomon, all these houses have the following in common;

- They were *built*

- They were built in the *chosen places*

- They were built by the *chosen builders*

- They were built using the *chosen materials*

- They were built according to *a pattern*

- They were built and *finished*

- They were finished and *furnished*

- Then they were *inhabited with glory*

The glorification of the houses was the last thing that happened before God accepted them. In other words, if the glory of God could inhabit it, God could inhabit it. If His Presence could accept it, His Person could accept it.

Enough cannot be said about the building of His house because revelation is still unfolding to flesh out all details, but suffice it to say that, today,

The house of God, the church, *is being built*

It is being built *in the earth*

It is being built *by Christ*—the Son with His sons

It is being built *using the sons*

It is being built for *His purpose*

It is *not yet fully finished*

It is *not yet fully furnished*

It is *not yet fully glorified.*

While saints continue to have a mental arrangement to depart the earth for heaven away in the sky, the great work of building this house in the earth gets slowed down and at times, has seemed to be grinding to a halt. But God shall not permit any failure; He shall have what He paid for fully. He shall have the house of His glory, built by Himself and ready for presentation to Himself by Himself for Himself.

His house built by His sons, using His sons shall fully emerge in the earth. To this company of sons He says,

> "we will come and make our home with him."
>
> John 14:23 nkjv

Even so, Father, let it be done. Amen.

CONCLUSION

While it is not lost on me that not all in the body of Christ who look forward to the coming of the Lord buy into the reality of restoration of all things before the Lord returns—ostensibly because the Bible says He is coming at an hour that no one knows about—we must bear in mind that to us who are the children of the light, He is not coming as a thief. In other words, we must not be caught unawares but knowing and prepared.

We must walk in revelation knowledge and fully prepare and expect His coming. The restoration of all things, in my understanding, is the restoration of all things "that must be restored" before He returns. By saying this, I mean the restoration of the devil is not included in the restoration of all things. It also means that not the whole human race shall be restored otherwise there shall be no judgment according to every one's works. Every teaching of the Bible must be contextualized so that proper meaning and interpretation are preserved and gleaned. God has a way of saying hard things in simple ways and so our finite minds must not shut the infinite God in and condition His unsearchable thoughts in the context of our realistic and practical minds.

Surely, Jesus could not have paid the ultimate price to present *any* church unto Himself. The Bible is clear: that "he might present it to himself a glorious church, not having spot, or wrinkle, or any such thing; but that it should be holy and without blemish". So instead of concentrating on the quantity of this kind of church, we need to concentrate on its quality.

Apostle Paul writes to the church in Colosse about the collective apostolic vision they had for the saints; "that we may present every man perfect in Christ". Col 1:28. How many are "every man?" That is none of our business. Our business is that whomsoever He gives to us, we must endeavor to preach Christ to that one, warning that one, and teaching that one in every wisdom, that we might finally achieve His vision in that one.

I believe that even when a literal number is given in the Book of Revelation about the number of those taken from every tribe of Israel, summing up to 144,000, God is not bound by the literacy of the figures but with the fullness of that number. When the fullness comes in, God knows.

So the Bible does not tell us how many species of animals existed at the time of the Flood, or how many in total came in: but we know that all that God wanted in came in. He knew when the fullness came in and He shut the door of the Ark. Our interpretation of numbers, figures, days, months, years and times, while gives a direction towards divine happenings, must be subjective to His sovereignty and deliberate manipulation and adjustments.

Indeed, there is a standard of quality, a threshold that the Scripture has set and Scripture cannot be altered, no matter how much it doesn't make practical sense to our human minds. I believe the buildings of God in the Old Testament have a lot to reveal about God's house in the New Testament.

When did the glory of God move in to become the Shekinah of God, dwelling among His people? Was it after *anything* was built *anyhow* by *anybody* using *anything* for God, or, was it after a piece of beautiful artistic work, done by the hands of chosen craftsmen with wisdom and diligence, using God's chosen materials and according to His pattern, was presented to God?

Why was Esther, though the graced one and chosen to be the king's queen, still kept away from the king for twelve months? Why did she undergo all the bathing and anointing, special diet and time, before she could be presented to the king? I believe the workers in the kingdom knew the quality of woman the king would have for a queen and time had to be taken to prepare the "purchased possession" of the king to make her meet for appearing before the king. After twelve months of preparation "with oils of myrrh ... with perfumes and preparations for beautifying women", then the woman would stand before the King, or better, would be presented to the king for actual marriage (Esther2: 1-18). So it is with the church, the Lord's Bride. John saw the church later in the Book of Revelation, appearing "prepared as a bride adorned for her husband" (Rev 21:2nkjv).

> "Let us be glad and rejoice and give Him glory, for the marriage of the lamb has come, and His wife has made herself ready."
>
> Rev 19:7nkjv

> ". . . for ye are the temple of the living God; as God hath said, I will dwell in them, and walk in them; and I will be their God, and they shall be my people. Wherefore come out from among them, and be ye separate, saith the Lord, and touch not the unclean thing; and I will receive you, and will be a Father unto you, and ye shall be my sons and daughters, saith the Lord Almighty."
>
> 2 Cor 6:16-18

> "Having therefore these promises, dearly
> beloved, let us cleanse ourselves from all
> filthiness of the flesh and the spirit, perfecting
> holiness in the fear of God."
>
> 2 Cor 7:1

As God's word is true, so we as sons of God in whom the Father plans to fully dwell and walk among, must become His chosen house of residence, taking all heed and doing all that is ascribed to us. Sons are the preferred dwelling place of the Father; the true definition of the house of God, the church.

As a company of saints moving in the spirit and power of Elijah, it is incumbent upon us to do as John the Baptist did, and then, do much more; because to us has the end of all things come. We must "make ready a people prepared for the Lord (Jesus)". Luke 1:17

The restoration of all things is primarily the sovereign working of God and extensively the incorporation of His sons in the earth.

FINAL PRAYER

Before you put down this book, kindly whisper this prayer from your heart and experience the essence and preeminence of sonship in your life, starting now;

"Loving, heavenly Father,
I thank You very much for opening my eyes to see
that becoming Your son
is Your divine design for me from the foundation of the world.

You predestined me
to the adoption as a son to Yourself by Christ Jesus
according to the good pleasure of your will.

Thank you Father,
for planning and designing
all this glorious relationship between You and me,
even before I was formed.

I have come to know,
that the best revelation I can ever have of You
is of a Father;
my Father which art in heaven,
and that
You sent Your only Begotten Son
to seek and save me from my fall
that I may be restored before You as a son, again.

Today,
I stand before You with this revelation;
that I was redeemed to become a son unto God.
I am a son of God.

Now Holy Father,
send the Spirit of Your Son into my heart,
that I may know You more deeply and intimately
as a Father
and relate with You
as a son
relates with his father.

You are my Father.
I am Your son
and Your preferred dwelling place.
Take away
all my fears, insecurities, indiscipline, confusion, bondage and
lack,
and in their stead,
bless me

with courage, security, identity, inheritance, discipline and
dominion.
Thank You Father.
I love You Father.

From today,
Lead me in my walk as a son
to cherish my position of relationship with and before You,
that makes me acceptable without works.
I no longer have to do to be.
I simply am a son and am accepted.
Thank You Father.
Lead me daily into Your rest and glory.
Amen".